"Vicar, there is in the midst of y
sheep. A character who, I am led
wastrel and a drunkard; an indolent man who neither
toils nor spins and yet, by nefarious means, finds
sufficient funds to fuel a demonic lust for alcohol."

Augustus Bamfylde, Curate.

OWD EDGAR

'*The Mayor of Grane*'

Some episodes in the life of Edgar Maudsley,
retired horsethief, whisky-spinner, liar,
drinker, poacher and blackmailer.

Published by
Millgate Publishing Ltd.,
48 Hall Carr Road,
Rawtenstall,
Rossendale,
Lancashire.
Tel. 0706 216380

Printed by
Nayler The Printer Ltd.,
Aero Mill,
Accrington,
Lancashire.
Tel. 0254 234247

Illustrations by Alastair Carter

CONTENTS

INTRODUCTION

Since the Owd Edgar stories began to be published in Red Rose Magazine, a number of questions have been asked which ought to be answered. First of all, the old man did exist, residing for many years at Heap Clough in Grane Valley. He died within living memory and many of those old enough, remember from their childhood days, seeing him walking around the Rossendale Valley, sack on back, collecting from the pavement odds and ends of whatever took his fancy. He did occasionally take paid employment, running errands for his neighbours and in summer would walk to Burnley to do some drystone walling, but of course, those who knew him best realised that the role of a semi-vagrant provided the perfect disguise for a whisky-spinner who needed to get to his customers unobtrusively.

As for his liking of beer and the quantities he consumed, the matter was best summed up by Edgar himself in the statement, *"Ah durn't sup as much as some folks think, mind thee, some folks do a gradely amount o' thinkin'."*

Regarding the actual stories of Owd Edgar, some are loosely based on known incidents in his life, others owe their existence to mere supposition, whilst the remainder have been inspired by personal visits to the pubs which the old man would have frequented.

It is possible that Edgar would not be too pleased by some of the things which have been written about him. On the other hand, he could be well satisfied, wherever he might be, that despite his uncouth ways and wickedness, he is remembered, whilst many others of his era, with all their airs and graces, remain forgotten.

Nick Dunnachie

25th April, 1991

A SIGN O' GOOD BEER

Edgar was the only customer in the Duke of Wellington, and as the landlady wanted to vent her feelings concerning her absent husband, it was the old man to whom she turned.

" 'E's a lazy, good for nothin' begger is that 'usband o' mine," she complained.

"Oh aye?" said Edgar.

"Aye 'e is an' all. Ah towd 'im to wash down t'cellar floor o' Monday, an' 'e didn't do it. Nor Tuesday, nor Wednesday, an' it's Thursday today, an' 'e still 'asn't done it. Ah reckon 'e must be as idle as thee."

Edgar resented that statement. It was true that he didn't have a regular job, but he kept himself busy enough. With a bit of thieving, a bit of poaching, some good clients for his whisky-spinning business, and a few other enterprises, he didn't do too badly for himself. He didn't dwell on this, or the insult he had just received. He was thinking. The old man had an ability to find peculiar ways of parting fools from their money and instinct told him that such an opportunity had presented itself. But how to go about it? What did he know about this woman and her husband? They had only been in the Duke for a few weeks. She was a little woman, a bit of sense about her, but a shrew. She was the boss, even though it was her husband's name over the door. The landlord, as she'd said, was lazy. He was also fat, stupid and greedy. Various images and possible future conversations went through Edgar's mind. 'Aye, it could work but Ah'd best be careful,' he thought.

"Givin' thee a problem then is it, t'cellar?" he asked.

"Reet enough it is. T'smell o' stale ale as yon great lump 'as spilt down theer is comin' up through t'floorboards," she answered.

"Ee 'eck. Nowt worse than funny smells in a pub. Bad for business is that," opined Edgar. The landlady politely refrained from commenting on the peculiar emanations which always accompanied Edgar. The old man finished his drink, put down his glass, and said, "Well, Ah must be off. Ah've spent up." He turned to go, then turned again, and resumed his place by the bar. "Mind thee, come to think on it," he said, looking the landlady right in the eye, "Ah reckon as Ah could persuade that 'usband o' yourn to clean out t'cellar every day for a month."

" 'Ow dost tha think tha could get 'im to do that?"

5

Edgar looked pointedly at the glass still on the bar. The landlady took the hint. She filled it. Edgar remained silent until he had the pint in his hand. In between gulps he said, "Let's put it this way, Ah'll bet thee 'alf a crown, as thy Tom'll wash out t'cellar every day for a month, startin' o' Sunday." Edgar put down the emptied glass. After a moment or two, the landlady had worked out that it would only cost her a penny a day, even if she lost the bet, which she doubted very much, knowing her husband. "Agreed," she said. "But 'ow are tha goin' to get 'im to do it?" "Leave that to me," replied Edgar." If things went as he expected, it would cost her money to find out.

Edgar often spent much of his time wandering up and down the narrow roads and cartways of the village. He liked to keep an eye on things and to see who was getting up to what. These little nuggets of information gleaned from his observations were, as far as his income was concerned, the icing on the cake. The begging and stealing and what have you provided him with enough money to keep out of the Workhouse. The knowledge he gained from his meanderings were used, as discreetly as possible, to persuade certain people that, should they give him a small amount of money for beer, their secrets would be safe with him. Most people, however, did not know of the cunning brain possessed by the old man. All they ever saw was a shabbily dressed character picking up discarded pieces of rubbish which were kept in a sack transported on the old man's back. It more than suited Edgar to be considered a harmless eccentric.

After his conversation with the landlady Edgar had to restrict his travels to the vicinity of the Duke. It was necessary for him to catch the landlord when he was on his own. Not an easy thing to do, considering his trade, but after a few false starts, Edgar achieved his aim.

"Mornin' Tom."

" 'Ow do, Edgar."

"Business alreet, is it?" Edgar enquired.

"Could be better, could be a lot better."

"Give o'er," replied Edgar, "Tha's plenty o' trade, an' o' top ov all that, tha's getten that reet good money spinner in thi cellar."

"What money-spinner?"

"Tha knows," insisted Edgar.

"What the 'eck are tha talkin' about?" The landlord was getting impatient. Edgar looked around to see if there was anyone listening. He knew there wasn't otherwise he wouldn't have started the conversation. Quietly, conspiratorially, he whispered hoarsely, "Tha knows, that frog. That frog in t'cellar."

"Ah knows nowt about no frog."

"Didn't t'last landlord tell thee about it then?"

"No 'e didn't. What about it?"

"Tell me," sighed Edgar, "Am Ah reet i' thinkin' as this is thi first pub?"

"Aye, but what about this frog?" The landlord had become interested.

"Well, chaps as 'ave bin i' t'trade for a bit know that if t'cellar's just cool enough and damp enough for a frog to live in, then th'atmosphere's just reet for t'storage o' beer. Keeps it i' perfect condition, like."

"What's all this got to do wi' a money-spinner i' mi cellar?" Edgar knew he had got the landlord where he wanted him.

"Well, thy cellar's getten a frog in it. But it's a reet special un. Th'owd landlord used to bet money wi' coach travellers, as 'e 'ad a frog down theer, as 'ud come out an' 'op about for 'im. Do a bit ov a jig, like."

"Ah durn't believe a word ov it!" exclaimed the landlord.

"It's true an' all, and it cost me a guinea to find out!"

This last statement from Edgar persuaded the man to believe him. Tom had heard quite a bit about Edgar, and to hear him admit that he had parted with money for anything other than beer, proved that he just couldn't be lying.

" 'Ow did 'e manage to get it to 'op around for 'im then?" he enquired.

" Nay, it cost me twenty-one shillin' to find that out," countered Edgar. "Any 'ow, Ah'd best be off. Ah'll be seein' thee," he said, taking a few paces down the road.

"Nay, wait a minute. 'Ang on. If Ah gi' thee thi money back, will tha tell me 'ow 'e got it to jump around for 'im?" pleaded the landlord. Edgar stopped in his tracks.

"Aye."

" 'Ere."

"Thanks."

" 'Ow?"

"Well, th'owd landlord used to go down to t'cellar wi' one o' them waterin' cans as 'as a rose on it. When 'e poured wi' it, it made a little shower o' water like, an' t'frog 'ud come out an' dance in it. But t'landlord reckoned as it were t'noise o' t'brush on t'floor as drew its attention first, so 'e used to sweep up, right vigorous like. 'E towd me as it took about a month or so for t'frog to get used to 'im."

"Ah think Ah'll 'ave a do at that," said the landlord. 'Quick an' easy money to be made,' he thought. With bets with all the passing trade, he'd soon have his guinea back and a whole lot more to boot. Edgar wandered off, his straight face masking the exuberance of his spirit.

The Duke had always been a calling place for the old man and during the following month, he enjoyed his visits even more. Things were going well for him. The landlord was doing all he could to entice the creature into the open, which greatly pleased his wife. "Ah can 'ardly believe it," she told Edgar on one of his occasional visits. " 'E's down theer two or three times a day, sometimes more. Dost know 'e's wore out two stiff brushes already?"

7

When the allotted time was up, the old man asked for his money, and the landlady gave it to him saying, " 'Ow did tha get 'im to do it? Acts all innocent wi' me, 'e does. Ah'd give anythin' to know what tha towd 'im?"

"Five shillin's, 'appen?" suggested Edgar.

"A shillin'," she offered. Half a crown was the sum settled upon. When it was safely in his pocket, Edgar told her the story he had spun for the landlord, and to protect himself in the future, he also told her about the guinea he had received from her husband.

"An' 'e believed it? The daft bugger 'as got more brass than brains!"

After a few more weeks, the landlord's enthusiasm for the frog began to wane. The landlady told Edgar this, complaining that the cleaning of the cellar had been missed. She asked him what she could do about it.

"Easy answer to that," said Edgar, looking meaningfully at his empty glass.

" 'Alf a crown's worth?" he smiled, expectantly.

The woman gave a rueful look as she placed the coin on the bar top.

"Reet," said Edgar, "Just make sure as it's thee as cleans t'cellar tomorrer. An' when tha comes up, tell 'im as a reet funny thing 'appened to thee. Tell 'im that as tha were pourin' some water out o' t'can this little frog 'ops out from nowhere, get's into t'spray o' t'water an' starts washin it's armpits."

" 'E won't believe that!" exclaimed the landlady. Then she saw the look on the old man's face. He gazed at her, his top lip over the bottom one and his eyebrows raised. "Aye, tha're reet, 'e will, the daft ninny."

On the following day the landlord listened to his wife's story with a mixture of amazement and jealousy. Having spent so long in a fruitless pastime, he had started to disbelieve Edgar's story, but the confirmation that there was a frog in the cellar renewed his faith and endeavours. Edgar was sure things could become very unpleasant for him if ever the landlady told her husband about the deception. But he was equally sure she would never do so, not whilst Tom was cleaning the cellar every day.

Occasionally, over the next decade or so, the landlord would tell Edgar that he had seen the frog, well, a glimpse of it at least. The man also reported these sightings to his wife, who didn't believe him in the least. But Edgar believed him. He saw a lot of frogs on his travels, and it was no trouble for him to pick one up now and again and secretly place it on the steps leading down to the cellar of the pub. Seeking the cool atmosphere, they would invariably hop downwards to be eventually discovered by the landlord who would say to himself, proudly, "A sign o' good beer is that."

A LASS FOR THE CURATE

"Bin a busy neet," said the landlord of the Holden Arms, hoping that the subtle hint would be sufficient to get the last customer out of the pub.

"Aye, Wick'un, tha'll o' coined some brass toneet, Ah'll wager," replied Edgar. He drained his glass and held it out to the landlord, whose smile of relief disappeared when the old man added, "Ah might as well gi' thee some more. Stick another pint i' theer."

The landlord did as he was bid, resigning himself to at least another ten minutes of the old man's company. He sighed as Edgar took a small sip of beer and placed the glass firmly on the bar top.

"If tha can't beat 'em, join 'em," muttered the landlord, pulling a pint for himself.

"Tha what?" asked Edgar.

"Ah said t'vicar's getten a new curate," said the landlord.

"So Ah've 'eard." Edgar stared into his beer.

"Ast sin 'im?" Wick'un asked.

"Not as Ah knows of."

"Ah wonder what 'e's like?" pondered the landlord. Whilst waiting for some response, he ambled round from behind the bar and started to sweep the floor where Edgar was standing. By Edgar's feet was a sack, Edgar's sack, the exact contents of which were known only to him, but it was generally understood that, among other things, it contained rotten fruit, meat and vegetables collected from the floor of the market after the stall-holders had left, but before the sweepers arrived. 'Clean meat never fattened a pig' was Edgar's philosophy on food.

" 'Ow would Ah know, if Ah've not sin 'im, tha daft bugger," came the retort, a long time in the making. The landlord ignored the remark for his attention had been drawn to the sudden appearance of a small animal which had popped its head out of Edgar's sack, taken a quick look at the surroundings and promptly disappeared from sight. The landlord glanced at Edgar to see if he had noticed anything, but the old man was staring into his glass.

'Should Ah tell 'im or not?' thought the landlord. 'If Ah tells 'im, God knows

9

what else 'e'll pull out ov 'is sack." He pointed his finger towards the floor and announced, "Thi sack's comin' open." Like a flash, Edgar's hand flew to the cord threaded through the top of the sack and pulled it tight. The landlord decided to go back to the subject of the curate.

"Ah've bin towd as 'e's a bit ov a firebrand."

"Oh aye?"

"Aye, keen as mustard so they say. Gettin' some reet good congregations." Edgar shook his head. "Well, tha won't find me joinin' 'em. Only ever bin in a church once in me life an' that were enough to put me off for good."

"When were that then? Christenin'?" the landlord hazarded a guess.

"No."

"Funeral?"

"No."

"Well, what then?"

"Leddin'."

"A weddin'?" said the surprised landlord, mis-hearing the word.

"No, leddin', Ah said. Up on t'roof. Ah'd getten a gradely sackful, hoisted it on me back and went straight through t'ruddy slates. Damn near brock me neck, Ah did. Tha won't catch me goin' in a church again." He paused before adding, "Come to think on it, Ah were lucky not to get catched then."

Not very far away, in the vicarage, the conversation revolved round the very subject of Edgar's irreligious behaviour. The curate had broached the matter by saying, "I have learned something today which I find most incredible. There is in the midst of your flock, a black sheep. A character who, I am led to understand, is a wastrel and a drunkard; an indolent man who neither toils nor spins and yet, by nefarious means, finds sufficient funds to fuel a demonic lust for alcohol."

"Someone has been telling you of Edgar Maudsley, I hope," said the vicar.

"You hope?" queried the curate.

"Very much so, for I wouldn't like two such men in the parish," retorted the vicar, though in all truth, he quite liked Edgar, which was more than he could say about the young man who sat by him. The services of the curate, Augustus Bamfylde, had been pressed on him by the bishop who had been impressed by the superficial charm and fawning nature which the fellow had displayed to His Grace but no other. The vicar had been unwell recently, and the bishop had sent his protege to assist him for two months whilst he convalesced. The curate had been with him for a week, but to the vicar, each day itself had seemed like a month. The young man was an over-sanctimonious, self-opinionated prig.

"You are correct in your assumption. It was indeed Edgar Maudsley to whom I referred," said the curate, waving his finger in the air. He continued, "We must bring this poor unfortunate back to the Fold." With a guile which Edgar

10

would have admired, the vicar persuaded the curate to view the matter of turning Edgar into a church-attending Christian, as a personal crusade, rather than a joint effort. The vicar had recognised the hopelessness of that particular cause many years ago, but he was extremely pleased by the increasing amount of enthusiasm displayed by the curate. No doubt the endeavour would keep him out of the vicar's sight, and in addition to which, any contact the curate might have with the old man would certainly prove to be disagreeable to him.

After several hours of listening to the curate's detailed account of how he would achieve his aims, the vicar, with feigned fervour, declared, "Your primary target, above all else, must be to keep him from the alehouses, taverns and beershops, for therein lies his iniquity."

"I will, I will," exulted the curate. 'That should keep you busy,' thought the vicar, before offering a silent prayer of thanks.

The third series of sharp raps on the door woke Edgar. He rose from his bed, shuffled to the window, flung it open and bawled, " Oo's makin' all that racket down theer? What dost tha want, this early in t'mornin'?"

"I am Augustus Bamfylde, curate, and I have come to talk to you," came the reply.

" 'Ang on theer. Ah'll be down i' toathry minutes," Edgar said in a more civilised tone. Suffering from a small hangover, he spent some time looking for his clothes before realising that he was still wearing them, hat and all. He sat on the edge of the bed and, whilst cleaning his teeth with his finger, tried to think of some reason for this unexpected visit.

"Buggered if Ah know," he concluded, got to his feet, went downstairs and opened the door.

" 'Ow can Ah 'elp thee, curate?" he asked.

"On the contrary, Mr. Maudsley," came the reply, "I am here to help you."

"Oh aye?"

"Yes indeed. I have come to help you see the light, to set your feet firmly on the path of righteousness, to save you from eternal damnation, to...." but Edgar interrupted the flow of words, " 'Oy, 'owd thi 'orses, come in an' sit thissen down." All of a sudden Edgar was pleased to see the curate, for anyone obviously so demented would surely be gullible enough to supply him with easy beer money. He led the way into the scullery and pulled out a chair from under the table.

"Theer." He gestured for the curate to take a seat. The latter did so, but with some reluctance, for almost directly under his nose, pinned to the table by a long bladed knife, was a dead rat.

"Tha were sayin'?" asked Edgar, who for the next hour listened to a monologue as to how the curate was going to convert his life. Before the visitor had left, Edgar had made certain promises, these being to attend church regularly, to forsake alcohol and to become respectably employed. Edgar intended to honour none of these vows, but the fact that he had made them seemed to please the curate. This made it far easier for the old man to 'borrow' five shillings from the curate in order that he could buy a new pair of trousers specifically for the purpose of attending the very next Communion.

On Sunday the curate waited with great anticipation for Edgar to arrive at the service, for he had wasted no time in telling the vicar of his rapid success in gaining the old man's promise. It was an embarassed curate who went in search of Edgar. He found him in the Holden Arms.

"You were supposed to be in church this morning."

"By gum, is it Sunday? Ah thowt it were only Friday."

"Didn't you hear the chiming of the bell?"

"Tha what?" asked Edgar, cupping his hand round his ear.

From that moment onwards the curate tracked Edgar religiously, noting his every movement. Each day, rising before dawn and retiring late at night, the curate succeeded in disturbing Edgar in every public house he entered. Many a time Edgar had given the young man the slip only to be caught in the act of drinking and to be soundly castigated for it.

" 'E's worse 'an one o' them Revenuer chaps," Edgar complained to the landlord of the Holden Arms, on one of the few occasions he had managed to temporarily elude his hunter.

" 'E's mytherin' me rotten, tha knows."

"Maybe so," replied the landlord, "but it's med thee reet popular wi' t'lasses." Edgar mulled on the observation. It was true. Ever since the curate had taken to pursuing him, the young ladies of the village had started to engage him in conversations which invariably included references to the curate.

'Aye, come to think on it,' thought Edgar, 't'young feller's not a bad lookin' chap an' gradely mannered where t'womenfolk is concerned. No wonder 'e's set a few 'earts a flutterin'. Bit bashful wi' t'young uns though. Ah reckon Ah ought to do summat about that.' The landlord interrupted his thoughts. "Art goin' to t'vicarage garden party o' Sunday?"

"Aye, Ah am," replied Edgar, who, to his astonishment, had been invited by the curate. A small grin split his face, and he exclaimed, "By 'eck, Wick'un, well done," for an idea had suddenly entered his mind how to give the curate 'summat else' to think about besides himself.

To put the idea into practice he needed the unwitting assistance of two girls from the village and decided that Alice Barnes would be most suitable. Big Ailse, as she was commonly known, was big, almost six feet tall, broad shouldered and strong enough to pull a plough. The other candidate would be Elizabeth Duckworth. As implied by her nickname, Betty Broom, she had a figure slender enough to be considered extremely gaunt. 'T'beauty o' them two is,' thought Edgar, 'both on 'em's as ugly as sin.'

Edgar started to put his plan into action on the following day. He well knew the inhabitants of the village and the routes they took on particular days. He contrived to meet Big Ailse, who, like many of the young women, had recently begun exchanging pleasantries with him.

"Mornin' Mr. Maudsley."

"Mornin' Alice."

" 'Ow are you today, Mr. Maudsley?"

"Fair to middlin', lass," said Edgar, at the same time thinking, 'As if tha cares.'

"Ah thowt Ah saw thee," started Alice, then quickly cleared her throat, before starting the sentence again. "I believe I saw you talkin' to the curate yesterday."

"Aye lass, tha did, an' Ah 'ope thy ears weren't burnin'."

Her eyes lit up. "Would they have reason to?" she asked, coyly.

"Oh aye lass."

" 'Ow's ta mean?" She whispered hoarsely, her galloping heart leaving behind any attempt at correct enunciation.

"Well, 'e particularly mentioned thee to me. " Oo's that fine strappin' lass oo's just gone past on t'other side o' t'road," he says. Them were 'is very words. An' then 'e says to me, "Ah 'ope she's comin' to t'vicarage garden party. Ah'd like, if possible, t'ave a few quiet words alone wi' 'er." That's what 'e said." All of this Edgar uttered with an air of confidentiality. Bright red, Big Ailse confirmed that she would indeed be at the vicarage garden party. Head flung back, she waddled off down the path, and as Edgar watched her go he noticed that her lumbering steps were occasionally interspersed with an ungainly skip. Within the hour Edgar had contrived a similar meeting with Betty Broom who also confirmed her intention to attend the gathering.

The important day arrived. The vicarage lawn was crowded. For once, Edgar sought out the curate. " 'Ow do, curate," beamed Edgar.

"You were not in church again this morning," the curate accused him.

"No Ah weren't but Ah think Ah've sin t'light o' what tha's bin tellin' me. Can we 'ave a quick chat inside t'vicarage. It's o' some importance to me."

The curate, eager to encourage Edgar's conversion, willingly agreed to meet him in the vicar's study in a few minutes time. Edgar wandered off, found Big Ailse and told her that the curate was waiting for her. Five minutes later he followed her into the vicarage. Stealthily, he crept upto the door of the study, pushed it open, and was delighted by the scene inside. Alice had the curate so securely pinned in her arms that a bullock would have had as much chance of escape. Intent on her devotions, she was oblivious to Edgar's presence. Not so with the curate, who, panic stricken by the occasion, was rendered speechless. He mouthed silently to Edgar for assistance, but the latter just nodded his head and went outside for another sandwich.

13

Twenty minutes later, the curate, in a state of great agitation, approached the old man. "It wasn't.. I didn't.. she thrust herself..," stuttered and stammered the curate. Edgar suggested that they should continue the conversation in the privacy of the vicar's study. They set off together, but Edgar got lost in the throng of people and the curate once again found himself alone in the study. Five minutes later there was a sharp knock on the door. Still fretful, the curate rushed to the door, saying as he opened it, "I've been waiting for you." He realised his mistake only a split second before two long, thin arms wrapped themselves tightly round his neck. From a horse-toothed mouth, only inches in front of his face, gushed the words, "An' Ah've bin waitin' for thee, curate." Though lathe-like in build, Betty's muscles were like thin rods of iron and the curate was forced into retreat until his back was pushed against the vicar's desk and he could go no further. "I'm sorry," he wailed, writhing ineffectively to free himself from her embrace. "I'm sorry, but I made a mistake!" "Nay, Mr. Bamfylde," cooed Betty, "there's no need o' confessions, though Ah'm glad to 'ear as tha's done a bit o' serious courtin', for Ah prefers chaps as 'ave 'ad a bit ov experience," thereby giving a hint of her state of chastity. The struggle continued, and whilst the curate desperately tried to disentangle himself, Betty kept up a constant flow of chatter as to the date of the nuptuals, who the bridesmaids would be, and various other details which she had spent the previous night planning. There was, however, one unfilled vacancy in the list of guests. "Oo's goin' to be thi best man?" she demanded, her left hand clutching a clump of his hair and pulling it backwards so that his head was barely an inch from the desk top. The curate's eye swivelled and rolled in panic and then came to rest on Edgar, who was standing silently at the door, his mouth agape.

"Mr. Maudsley!" cried the curate, stretching out his free arm towards the old man. "By gum," said Betty, with some admiration, shaking her head and smiling at the same time, "Tha're a crafty un, aren't tha? Tha'd do owt to get that owd chap into church." The curate's eyes flitted away from the door to stare aghast into the face of the girl holding him down. He looked again towards the door and was more than slightly dismayed to see that he and Betty were once again alone in the room.

The curate eventually disentangled himself from Betty's embrace and went in search of Edgar who he found in a quiet corner of the garden.

"I must explain to you that there has been a great misunderstanding," he spluttered. "I can assure you I did nothing to encourage them."

"O' course tha didn't," agreed Edgar. "Ah'll believe that, but then again it'll be a different story when their fathers find out. Which on 'em does tha fancy marryin' t'most?"

"Marry?" squealed the curate, who had intentions of a bishop's daughter at the very least.

"Aye, marry," replied Edgar. "Ah can tell thee, they're not reet keen on chaps as are philanderers round 'ere. An' goodness knows what t'vicar'll say."

"The vicar?"

"Aye, 'e'll be none too pleased when Ah tells 'im."

"You? Tell the vicar?"

Edgar slowly shook his head as he spoke. "Well, it's me duty as a prospective Christian as Ah should tell t'truth and be 'onest in all things. Tha towd me so thissen. Then again, as Ecclesiastes puts it, chapter ten, verse nineteen, 'a feast is med for laughter and wine maketh merry but money answereth all things.' Now theer's a thought." So saying, Edgar brushed the palm of one hand with the fingers of the other, and it dawned on the curate that in some way, Edgar had engineered the events of the day in order to blackmail him. He grabbed hold of the old man's lapels and snarled, "Woe to them that devise iniquity!" Edgar caught hold of the curate's wrists and quickly quoted, "Ecclesiastes, chapter seven, verse nine, 'Be not hasty in thy spirit to be angry for anger resteth in the bosom of fools.'" The young man, realising that he was drawing the attention of some of the other guests, released his grip and made as if he were merely smoothing a few wrinkles from the old man's coat.

By Monday night things were, as far as Edgar was concerned, back to normal. A pint in his hand and his elbow resting on the bar at the Holden Arms. The curate, on advice from Edgar, had packed up his things and left the village for good. He'd also left behind several broken hearts and a guinea now resting in Edgar's pocket. Alongside it was a further ten shillings, a gift from the vicar who had guessed that Edgar had had something to do with the premature departure of his assistant. The landlord leaned over the bar and commented, "Tha're lookin' fair chuffed wi' thissen, Edgar."

"Aye Wick'un, Ah am, reet chuffed, Ah can tell thee," beamed the old man.

"Go on then, tell us," said the landlord, who, although he had heard of the curate's hasty disappearance, was not acquainted with the reason.

"Nay, Ah can't do that, Wick'un. As it says in t'good book, 'a tale bearer revealeth secrets, but 'im that's ov a faithful spirit concealeth t'matter,' Proverbs, chapter eleven, verse thirteen."

"Just this once, Ah'll take thi word on it," replied the landlord.

A POUND O' FLASH

Edgar was feeling content with his morning's endeavours. Since breakfast he had gained a new customer for his personally distilled whisky, picked up a goodly amount of discarded vegetables, barely bruised and only a little rotted, and finally, to his great delight, had found a shilling on the pavement. The silver discovery ended his working day and at twelve o' clock he entered the Holden Arms for what he considered a well-deserved drink. Despite his fondness for beer, Edgar strongly disapproved of drinking at dinner-time but as usual he assuaged both his conscience and his thirst by refraining from ordering full pints and settling for halves instead. After a number of these, he pondered, not for the first time, how it could be that two halves, although cumulatively the same as a pint, and ordered separately to boot, always seemed to be consumed in less time.

"Want another un in 'ere?" asked Wick'un, the landlord, picking up Edgar's empty glass.

"Aye, go on then, just an 'alf."

"Celebratin', are we?" enquired Wick'un whilst filling the glass for the tenth time.

"Celebratin'? Me, celebratin'?" said Edgar, with a tone of utter surprise in his voice. He scratched his ear, neck and armpit, placed his elbows on the bar, picked up his glass and with a mournful groan, muttered, "Drownin' me sorrows, that's what Ah'm doin'."

"That meks two o' thee then," whispered Wick'un, indicating with a quick glance, a customer who had been sitting in the tap room but was now standing next to Edgar. The old man twisted round on his stool to get a better view of his neighbour, who by the cut of his clothes, gave the appearance of being well-to-do. Edgar was surprised to see someone of society in such a place as the Holden Arms, and was intrigued as to the circumstances which had brought the young man hither. Edgar casually inspected him for the following five minutes, in which time, Young Flash, as Edgar had dubbed him, looked nervously at his watch seven times, and had ordered and drunk three large brandies.

"Waitin' for someone?" Edgar enquired. Normally, it would have been highly

16

unlikely for the young man to converse with the likes of Edgar. However, things were not normal and the old man received a carefully enunciated reply. "No, I am not waiting for someone, I am waiting for a train, a train to Liverpool, and from there I shall set sail to America where I shall make my fortune."

"If tha don't mind me sayin' so, tha'd appear to be worth a bob or two already," said Edgar.

"I have but what I wear and a hundred pounds," offered the young man, most indiscreetly in Edgar's opinion, and in the time it took for the old man to pick up his drink and take a sip, he had formulated a two pronged attack on Young Flash's wallet. Slowly he put down his glass and said, with a solemn air, "It's funny that tha should mention the word fortune. Ah tells fortunes."

"Is that so?" asked the young man.

"Aye," said Edgar.

"What method do you use?"

"Ah reads palms," Edgar replied, studying his own for effect.

"Do you really?"

"Aye," said Edgar. "Dost want me to...?" completing the sentence by pointing his finger to the young man's hand.

"Why not?" came the response, and Edgar knew that the first stage of his plan was as good as completed. He took hold of the proffered hand, saying, "Let's 'ave a look an' see what fate 'as in store for thee." He studied the hand, both back and front, not so much for reasons of palmistry, but more to enviously eye the heavy gold signet ring adorning the third digit.

"Well, what can you see?" demanded the young man.

" 'E can see that tha's getten four fingers an' a thumb," said Wick'un, who had been in close proximity ever since Edgar had started talking to his potential victim. The old man looked up and gave Wick'un a faint smile, then resumed his study for a few seconds more before starting his interpretation.

"Tha sees that line theer," he said, pointing to no particular part of the hand, "that means that tha're definitely goin' to make a long sea voyage."

"Any numbskull could say that," interrupted Wick'un. " 'E's already towd thee that."

"Nay, 'e didn't," responded Edgar. " 'E towd us as 'e were settin' off on one. Ah'm sayin' as 'e'll get to t'other side."

"Go on," said Wick'un, scornfully.

"Yes, please tell me more," added the young man, sincerely.

"Reet enough," said Edgar. "Tha see thi love line theer, 'ow it bumps across t'line o' fortune, by 'eck, it's interestin' is that, it tells a tale does that."

"It's not th'only one," muttered the landlord.

"Do tell me what it says," pleaded the innocent dupe.

"Well, the way Ah sees it is this. There's bin money i' thi life already, but look, t'line o' fortune's good enough now, but it breaks 'ere for a short spell then crops up again o'er theer, gettin' deeper an' wider till it spreads out all o'er t'show. By thump, tha're goin' to do well in America. What wealth tha's 'ad before thi long journey, compared to what tha'll 'ave later on, it's like comparin' a brooklet wi' a ragin' torrent."

"What a load o' mumbo jumbo," sneered Wick'un and Edgar could see from the young man's face that he was somewhat inclined to agree with the landlord. "Maybe, maybe not," said Edgar, surprisingly without a hint of malice. He peered more closely at the palm. "It says 'ere as there's a woman involved an' all, a good lookin' lass, tha were close to 'er, 'appen engaged, but 'ey up, there's a problem. Someone in authority says, "No." A big man, powerful, forbids marriage. "Out o' th' question," he says. An' that's why tha're goin' away." Edgar looked up to see what effect this last statement had, and was pleased, judging from the look on Young Flash's face, that he had hit the nail on the head. Stunned by the accuracy the young man hoarsely uttered, "Absolutely amazing. My position exactly." Wick'un was also greatly impressed, though it is unlikely that he would have been, had he known what means Edgar had really used to give accuracy to his divination. The truth of the matter was that Edgar, whilst on his travels, had recently heard of a forbidden liason between a certain young lady, daughter of a Methodist, and a young gentleman, by the name of George Edwin Ratcliffe, son of a wealthy Anglican. The opposing religions created a barrier which neither father wanted to be breached. Edgar, on seeing the initials GER engraved on the young man's signet ring had recalled a servant's tittle tattle and put two and two together.

Although well pleased with the effect of his prophesy, Edgar wasn't too certain whether this alone would be sufficient to loosen Young Flash's purse strings. Step two in his plan was to gain some degree of sympathy for himself. "Thi father forbid thee from gettin' wed, did 'e?" he asked the young man, who nodded his head sadly.

"Fathers can be cruel things," Edgar stated. "Ah remember, as if it were yesterday, when Ah were a lad, an' me father took me to t'mill, up to t'top floor, three stories 'igh it were. 'E sits me on t'pulley beam an' says, "Son, stay theer," an' 'e went downstairs an' out into t'courtyard. Then 'e looks up at me, an' 'e says, "Reet son, jump."

"Nay father," Ah says, "Ah'll hurt missen."

"Come on son, jump. Ah'll catch thee," 'e says.

"Nay, 'appen tha'll drop me an' Ah'll suffer some scathe," Ah tells 'im.

"Would Ah drop thee?" says father. "Would Ah drop me only son on t'floor? Nay lad, jump."

Edgar shook his head at the memory. "An' 'e 'eld 'is arms out so Ah leapt off, an' as soon as Ah'd let go an' were flyin' through th'air, Ah saw 'im step back an' put 'is 'ands in 'is pockets. Well, Ah 'it t'floor wi' a reet thwack, an' 'e looks down at me does father, an all 'e says is, "That's thi first lesson i' life son, durn't trust anyone." Edgar sucked his moustache, waiting for the inevitable comment. Aghast, the young man asked, "And did you suffer injury?"

"Aye," replied Edgar, gently slapping his thigh. "Me legs, tha know." He heaved a sigh, at the same time casting an eye at the clock. "Tha'd best be off in a minute, or tha'll miss thi train," he said. "Ah must say, it's bin a reet pleasure talking to such a sensible young chap as thissen. Ah wish thee all th' best o' luck in America." Edgar dropped a paternal hand on the innocent's shoulder, and then, before any response could be given, he twisted round in his seat to greet a giant of a man who had just walked into the pub. "Tim, come 'ere a minute will ti?" Nature had been generous to Tim o' Bob's, not only as to his physique, but also his temperament, and it was well known that he was a most obliging man. " 'Ow do, Edgar, what's ta want?" he asked.

"Pick me up an' carry me into t'privvy," commanded Edgar. "Aye alreet," said Tim o' Bob's , as if the instruction was an everyday occurence. He bent over, put one arm under Edgar's legs, and hoisted him into the air.

"Nay lad, stool an' all," Edgar said very gently, as if Tim had forgotten the simplest part of a regular routine. Tim put the old man back on the stool, adjusted his hands and lifted again. He started to move towards the back door, but Edgar gave another instruction. " 'Ang on a second, Ah'll just leave me 'at theer," he said, putting his trilby on the bar top, brim upwards.

"Reet lad, lead on."

"Ah can't do that, tha're i' front o' me," replied Tim.

"Just walk us into t'privvy, Tim, theer's a good chap." Tim started to move, and as he did so, Edgar looked over his shoulder and called out, "Good day to thee young sir, Ah doubt as tha'll see me again."

"Thank you most kindly," replied the young man with a small tear in his eye, as Edgar was transported through the door leading to the backyard. He then turned to the landlord and said, "What a courageous old man he is, to bear with such fortitude the vicissitudes of life."

Wick'un, not having a dictionary to hand, merely nodded his head in agreement, in the hope that it was the correct gesture. Another customer called out for his attention and he was drawn to the other end of the bar. The young gentleman looked at his watch and announced, "Landlord, I must be on my way. My thanks for your hospitality, and please, if you will, convey my regards to the old man." He fumbled in his pocket, pulled out a piece of paper and slipped it into the lining of the hat on the bar. He completed the manoeuvre without, so he thought, being observed by the landlord, whose back was turned. Wick'un, however, had made good use of the mirror behind the bar. He turned to the young customer, "Bin a reet pleasure an' Ah sincerely 'opes tha finds 'appiness in Americky. Bon voyidge." He watched the emigrant go through the front door and then casually sidled over to Edgar's hat to see what had been placed inside it.

Edgar, who had been keeping a close eye on the proceedings through a crack in the partially open back door, beat Wick'un to the hat by a fraction of a second, the same length of time which it took to transfer whatever had been placed in it to the depths of a long pocket.

"What were that?" Wick'un asked.

"Nowt," replied Edgar.

"Liar," said Wick'un.

"A ten shillin' note," whispered Edgar.

"Liar," Wick'un repeated, but louder.

"A pound," Edgar mouthed.

"Then tha ought to be flamin' well ashamed o' thissen," Wick'un reprimanded him. "Tellin' such a tale, an' pretendin' to be afflicted like that. It were cruel."

" 'Ey, it would a bin crueller still, if 'e'd seen me walk into t'pub an' 'adn't let on until after Ah'd gone through all me 'istrionics. Just think, all that effort would o' gone to waste." Edgar abhorred waste. "Any'ow," he continued, "it were just a bit ov a joke, that's all." But he could see that the landlord was still displeased with him. "Ah suppose," he suggested dubiously, "Ah suppose Ah could run after 'im an' give 'im is brass back."

"Thee?" cried the landlord. "Run after someone to give 'em their money back?"

"Well," said Edgar. "Maybe best not, not i' this case. 'E might think it's some sort o' miracle."

"We'd all think it were some sort o' miracle, let alone 'im!" snapped the landlord. Edgar thought it best to change tack. " 'Ey, Ah did give 'im fair warnin', tha knows."

"Tha did?"

"Aye. Ah towd 'im not to trust anyone." Edgar shook his head slowly. "Ah fear as that young feller'll not 'ave much ov 'is 'undred pound left by t'time 'e gets t'America, if 'e meets another ninety-nine chaps like me."

Wick'un stared at Edgar, then leaned towards him so that their faces were but a few inches apart. "Edgar, if that feller were to travel t'Americky an' back a score o' times, Ah doubt as if 'e'd meet one other chap like thee, let alone another ninety ruddy nine!"

Edgar considered this comment for a moment. Slowly, his back straightened and a smug smile settled on his lips. Never had he been so complimented, and before he could prevent himself, the question came out, "Wick'un, would'st care t'ave a drink wi' me?" The landlord, dumbfounded, could only nod his head. Edgar, immediately regretting the unpremeditated offer, sought to limit the financial loss by adding, "Just an 'alf, mind."

A GAIN IN THE PUB

Edgar was forced to move his hand from his mouth in order to call out to the landlord of the Holden Arms, "Oy, Wick'un, stick another pint i' theer." He clutched his mouth again, grimacing from agony.

"Still sufferin' from toothache, are we?" asked Wick'un.

"Aye, t'pain's murderin' me," came the reply.

"Which un is it?" enquired the landlord. Edgar carefully lifted his hand, snarled his upper lip and pointed a finger to his eye-tooth. Wick'un peered closely into Edgar's mouth.

"That un?" he asked, at the same time, and none too gently, tapping the offending tooth with the stub of a pencil. Edgar shot six inches into the air and roared an unrepeatable epithet. Tim o' Bob's, a kindly soul, standing next to Edgar, admonished him, "Ee, Edgar, that's not th' sort o' language as tha should be usin' o' Christmas Eve."

"Absolutely reet," Wick'un agreed, beaming with pleasure. "Besides which, Ah towd thee a fortneet ago as tha should go an' see a doctor or one o' them dentical chaps. Get it tekken out and be done wi' it."

"That'd cost me some brass, would that," complained Edgar.

"Well, tha ought to do summat about it," said Tim o' Bob's.

"Aye, 'appen tha could put in for a visit from t'Tooth Fairy, 'stead o' Santa Claus," suggested the landlord.

In fact, Edgar had done several things about it; he had tried laudanum, but the smell and taste of it were unpleasant, even to his unfastidious palate; he had tried bathing the tooth in whisky but to no effect, though this was partly due to the fact that the liquor didn't stay long enough in his mouth to give any benefit; and he had also tried consuming copious amounts of beer. The last, although not dispelling the agony, at least helped him to fall asleep more easily when he retired for the night. The time for bed however, was several hours away, and in the meantime, Edgar thought that a conversation based on some topic other than his suffering and woe, might not be a bad thing. His present company, one innocently, the other maliciously, were enjoying themselves at his expense. He looked around for someone else to talk to. He had a wide choice, for it seemed that every man in the village had forsaken his home and his part in the hustle and bustle of the last minute preparations for the following day, in favour of a quiet celebratory drink at the Holden Arms. Edgar stood on his stool, the better to see over the, by now, well-celebrated multitude.

"There's summat goin' on i' theer," he stated, jerking his head towards the tap-room." " 'Ow's ta mean?" asked Wick'un, who, had he been perfectly sober, would have noticed for himself that a virtual silence had descended on the room, which until a few minutes before, had been filled with boisterous shouts of encouragement from the men crowded inside.

"Not reet noisy, is it?" elaborated the old man.

"Now tha comes to mention it, it 'as gone a bit quiet i' theer. Let's 'ave a gander," Wick'un proposed. He lifted the bar-hatch and set off to investigate, closely followed by Edgar and Tim o' Bob's.

The object of attention in the tap-room was a game of three card brag, a gambling game, played with cards, in which the best, and unbeatable hand, is three threes. Six men were sitting round an oblong table, four of whom had thrown in their hands, the two still in the game clutching their cards close to their chests. Between them, in the centre of the table was the pot, consisting of a large pile of coins, several notes of the realm and various pieces of paper.

"Tha knows me rules, no gamblin'," announced Wick'un.

"Shtuff thi rules," said one of the contenders.

"We'll finish after thish 'and," said the other.

"Aye, let 'em finish," came a call from one of the onlookers, followed by other mutterings in support of that motion.

"Alreet," said Wick'un, reluctantly. "Get on wi' it then. Oo's turn is it?"

"It'sh up to 'im," said the first player.

" 'Ang on, wait thi sweat, Ah'm thinkin'," said the second.

"What's there to think on?" asked the first.

"Ah'm thinkin'," said his opponent, very slowly, "what else Ah can bet wi'. Now, Ah've done me 'ouse, 'aven't Ah?"

"Aye, it's theer," confirmed the first, pointing a finger towards one of the pieces of paper which lay on the table.

"What's this?" exclaimed Wick'un, snatching up the slips. With some difficulty, he read aloud the inscriptions. "I.O.U. pair o' clogs, five shillin's. I.O.U. chest of drawers in parlour, fifteen shillin's. I.O.U. 12 Gas Street, fifty pounds." Wick'un quickly flicked through the rest of the I.O.U.'s. "Tha's both bet thi 'ouses."

"That's reet," said the first player. Wick'un asked him, "What'll 'appen if tha loses, tha'll be livin' in 'is 'ouse, won't tha?"

"Aye, but Ah won't lose, an' that means as 'e'll be livin' i' mine. But not for long, cos Ah'll be throwin' t' miserable beggar out onto t' street tomorrer." This received the reply, "Ah'll not be movin', cos Ah've got a better 'and than thee. It'll be thee that'll be flittin', an' bugger tomorrer, Ah'll be 'avin' thee out bi midneet."

"Tha're both daft i' th'eads," pronounced an exasperated Wick'un, at a loss as how to resolve the situation. However, whilst he had been talking to the two men, Edgar had taken a stroll round the table. He returned to the landlord's side, nudged him and gave a wink.

"Tell us, Jack," Edgar asked the first player. " 'Ow much rent does ta pay?"

"Four an' six a week, if its owt to do wi' thee," came the reply.

22

Edgar turned to the other player. "An' 'ow much is thy rent, Fred?"

"Five an' six a .... Blummin' Harry, t'landlord 'ud not be reet suited if 'e knew we were gamblin' wi' 'is 'ouses."

"This landlord's not reet suited that tha's gamblin' at all," snapped Wick'un picking up the two I.O.U.'s referring to houses and ripping them into pieces. Out of the corner of his mouth he whispered, "Thanks Edgar."

In a similar fashion, the old man responded, "Tha's still getten a bit ov a problem to sort out."

"Tha what?" asked Wick'un.

" 'Ow many treys are there in a pack o' cards?" enquired Edgar, nodding at the table top. Wick'un picked up the rest of the pack from the table and carefully went through it. He found five threes which he showed to Edgar.

"That's interestin', is that," whispered the old man. "Particularly as they've getten three apiece an' all."

Wick'un cheerfully announced this news to the thirty or so men crowded into the small room and proved his statement by snatching the cards from the two players and holding them up for all to see. Guffaws of laughter rent the air, and increased when the two men began to accuse each other of cheating. They stood up, reached over the table and grabbed hold of one another by the lapels.

Normally Edgar kept out of other people's fights, but on this occasion he surprised everyone by trying to intervene. He clasped the men's arms as if to stop them from being able to strike one another. His involvement in the struggle only added to the mayhem and the card table was knocked over, sending the pile of money onto the floor. Coins flew, bounced and rolled in all directions. Whilst the landlord, with the aid of Tim o' Bob's, separated the antagonists, everyone else scrambled to pick up the coins and notes, all of which were replaced on the table with the exception of five shillings which Edgar had deftly slipped into his pocket.

"Now then," commanded Wick'un, "let that be an end to it, or go outside an' sort it out between thissen." He picked up the money from the table and gave them a rough half portion each."

" 'E were cheatin'," said Fred.

"So were thee," said Jack.

"Aye, but tha were cheatin' more."

"Ah were not!" The argument flared up again, and the two men resolved to settle their differences by means of a clog-fight. They staggered out into the cold night air, closely followed by a large body of men all keen to witness the event, some carrying lanterns to illuminate the contest.

"It's barbaric is this," declared Wick'un.

"Not as barbaric as what it replaced," commented Edgar. "When Ah were a lad, they used to get stuck in, tooth an' nail, an try to gouge each other's eyes out." He sucked his breath in at the memory of one such bout he had witnessed.

This action was a mistake, for the cold atmosphere hit the nerve end of his tooth, sending a shock of pain through his entire jaw. He groaned.

"Tha ought to do summat about that tooth," said Wick'un.

The spectators formed a circle round Jack and Fred, who took hold of each other's shoulders in preparation for the battle to come. Heeled and soled with strips of iron, clogs as footwear provided many a Lancashire working man with a pair of deadly weapons. A well-aimed kick could crack a man's shinbone or put his kneecap on the back of his leg. Such a blow could decide the contest and therefore, it was not unusual for the assailants to commence warily, shifting their feet a few inches, feinting and threatening without making a serious lunge. There again, it was not unusual for the combatants to start lashing out straightaway, regardless of the consequences. Edgar unofficially started the contest, "Blest is 'e oo's quarrel's just, thrice blest is 'e oo gets 'is blow in first."

Fred and Jack started well enough, twisting each other round, tugging gently on their arms, feet dancing and stepping, both of them trying to find an opening. This action continued for several minutes, amidst a growing barrage of catcalls and jeers from the spectators who were getting cold. Finally though, Jack stood stock-still for a second, usually a fatal error, took the time to say, "Oh bugger this," and swung back his right leg as if to take a swipe at a football. His left leg, weakened by drink, failed to do its duty to support the beer-filled body, and Jack fell tumbling to the ground, dragging Fred down onto him. As the two men struggled to their feet, Wick'un whispered to Tim o' Bob's, who disappeared into the pub.

The fight continued with the combatants holding each other by the neck, in a fashion more romantic than aggressive. Fred attempted a kick, but again, three legs proved to be insufficient support for the two men, and again they fell to the floor in an untidy heap, both shouting curses and claiming victory. At this moment Tim o' Bob's reappeared, carrying in the one hand a bucket of beer, and in the other, two pint glasses. Wick'un took these from the young giant and asked him to pick up the drunken men. Tim o' Bob's did as he was told, by stooping at the waist, getting hold of them by the scruff of their necks and straightening his back. He stood quite nonchalantly, arms outstretched, in each hand a drunk, both of whom were clear of the floor by a good twelve inches. Mutterings of admiration came from the onlookers, for any demonstration of strength by Tim o' Bob's was worth seeing, and also good for a tale at a later date.

The chance of a better tale quickly followed, for Jack, now that his legs were free from the necessity of supporting his body, made use of their liberty by swinging a long and well-aimed punce at the giant's leg. Jack's right clog iron had travelled almost two yards and was moving fast when it came into contact with Tim's right kneecap. A terrific crack rent the air, the spectators gasped and winced with sympathy. Open-mouthed, they waited for the response.

Tim's figure remained upright. He turned his head to Jack, now petrified with fear, as the realisation of what he had done sank into his brain. He, like everyone else present, knew of the giant's good nature, but even so, all of them expected violence. Tim had made his mark some years before when, as a fourteen year-old, he had thrown a grown man over an eight foot wall for mistreating a donkey. The spectators looked around to see which wall would be most suitable for a repeat of this performance, but Tim o' Bob's remained his amicable self, and the only retribution the captive suffered was a gentle mid-air shake accompanied by the admonition, "Stop playin' silly beggars, Jack."

Under Wick'un's instructions, the two men were transported into the barn and dumped on the floor where they lolled helplessly against each other. The landlord pushed the bucket of beer between them, dipped the glasses into it and thrust one each into the men's hands. "Come closer wi' that lantern," he ordered Edgar, and then slipped his hand into the drunk's pockets and took out some money as payment for the beer. "Another eight pints apiece should see thee both reet, one way or t'other," he said to the recumbent figures and then said to Edgar and Tim, "Come on, let's get back i'side." Edgar waited until Wick'un's back was turned before quickly filling his own glass from the bucket. The trio walked back into the warmth of the pub and Wick'un resumed his usual place behind the bar. "Oo in their reet mind 'ud be a flippin' landlord," he muttered.

"Me for one, if Ah could sell beer at ten bob a gallon," replied Edgar, who had seen how much Wick'un had extracted from the men's pockets. The old man grinned, an expression soon replaced by a grimace as the aching tooth sent out a jolt of pain.

"Tha ought to do summat about that tooth," said Wick'un.

"So tha keeps tellin' me," replied Edgar.

"Ah'll buy thee a pint, if tha thinks it'd 'elp," offered Tim o' Bob's.

"Ah think it would," said Edgar.

"Set 'em up, Wick'un," said Tim, gesticulating a drinking motion with his arm. Before he lowered it, he started to turn towards Edgar who was standing behind him, with the intention of asking him if a whisky would be more preferable. He'd got as far as saying, "Wouldst tha..." by which time his elbow had got as far as Edgar's mouth. The force of the blow knocked the old man through a crowd of drinkers and he disappeared from view, leaving behind him two thin furrows in the sawdust on the floor, scraped out by the heels of his clogs.

"Whoops," said Tim o' Bob's.

Edgar reappeared clutching a tattered rag to his mouth.

"Tha great, gormless, clumsy bugger, tha damn near took me 'ead off me shoulders," he howled. The eyes of every man in the pub were on him as he ranted and raved, shaking his fist under the giant's nose.

25

"Ah've a good mind to..." he paused as he tried to think of what physical damage he could inflict, which gave Wick'un the chance to make the comment, "Ah see that tha's done summat about yon tooth." Edgar probed the inside of his mouth with his tongue and discovered a gap where the aggravating tooth had been. "Well done, lad, well done." Edgar clapped Tim o' Bob's on the shoulder. "Ah'd almost made me mind up to go an' see t'doctor next week, and get the little begger drawn. Tha's saved me a shillin'." This announcement caused some hilarity and Edgar admonished those who'd laughed, by saying, "It's not funny tha knows, tha should remember as a penny saved is a penny earned." He inspected the rag he had been holding to his mouth and found in it the tooth which had recently vacated its position. "Well now, look at that," he said, holding it up. "Now Tim, what were tha sayin' about buyin' me a pint?" Tim gave him a querying look and studied the molar in Edgar's hand before replying, "Well, Ah were goin' to buy thee a pint for thi tooth like, but it's out now." "Aye, true enough," Edgar agreed, and thrust the fang into Tim's hand, adding, " 'Ere's thi tooth, wheer's me pint?"

For the first time in more than a fortnight, Edgar drank purely for pleasure rather than pleasure and necessity combined, and it was a very drunken old man who crawled into bed some hours later. In the course of reaching out to extinguish the oil-lamp, he noticed the glint of something silver in one of the turn-ups of his trousers which he had cast onto the floor by the bedside. He discovered it to be a sixpenny piece, which unbeknown to him had been one of the many coins scattered from the card table earlier in the evening. He went to sleep clutching it in his left hand.

It was nearly midday when Edgar woke up with the sensation of a hundred horses galloping around in his skull. He suspected that something was wrong and after a moment or two realised what it was. The source of the pain was in the top of his head, whereas it should have been in his mouth. He ran a dry and almost senseless tongue around his mouth. The tooth had gone. He opened his eyes in surprise, and was even more astonished to see, in his hand which rested on the pillow, a sixpenny piece. He asked it, "Where the 'eck did tha come from?" but received no reply. He tried to recall the events of the previous night, and vaguely remembered a clog fight. He ran his right hand down his legs to his feet. His legs were still there, intact and without pain, so it was doubtful he had been involved in that. He searched his mind for any other memories, but without success. A complete blank, not a single hint or clue as to what else had transpired.

"Now wheer did me tooth go, and wheer did tha come from?" he enquired again of the coin in his hand. A small thought raised itself in his mind, and despite his hangover he chuckled at the impossibility of the idea. A visit from the Tooth Fairy indeed. But he wished it Merry Christmas all the same.

SAMMY SUP-ALL'S FOOT-IN

Edgar stamped the snow from his clogs, pushed open the door to the Holden Arms and stomped up to the bar.

"Wick'un, where are ti?" he bawled.

"Ah'm in 'ere," came the reply. Edgar peered in through the tap-room door and saw the landlord, coat-tails lifted, warming himself at the fire.

"It is a bit cowd, in't it?" said Edgar, walking across the room to join his host.

" 'Utch o'er a bit," adding a nudge of the elbow to the request. The landlord yielded a few inches of fire-space.

"It's a gradely fire is yon," remarked the old man.

"It ud be a sight more gradely if there were a dozen chaps warmin' their backsides against it, instead o' just thee an' me," replied the landlord.

"Aye, it does seem a bit on t'quiet side," observed Edgar.

"Quiet? Quiet?" wailed the landlord, "Apart from me an' thee an' t'dog, t'pub's empty. Where is everbody, eh? Answer me that, if tha will. No need to tell me. Ah can tell thee where they all are. Keepin' out ov all this snow, that's where they all are. It's ruinin' me trade is all this bad weather. Dost know, it's not stopped snowin' sin' Christmas?" The landlord lapsed into a morose silence. Edgar knew only too well that for the past month every day had brought with it a fresh fall of snow. A large part of his diet came from the floor of the local market, but the slush churned up by boot and clog made it difficult for him to find and retrieve discarded meat and vegetable matter. He looked down at his sack lying limp and empty at his feet. Usually by this time of day it would have been at least half filled with foodstuffs, bits of timber for the fire and other odds and ends. If the weather did not improve soon he would have to start buying food.

" 'Appen things'll buck up in a day or so," he said, hopefully.

"Not a ghost ov a chance," replied Wick'un. "This winter's goin' to be long an' 'ard." He sighed, "By 'eck, Ah'd do owt for just a week o' good trade." As an afterthought he added, "It wouldn't be so bad if Ah could just get some o' them beggars in oo ran up a fair-sized slate o'er Christmas."

"Neither a lender nor a borrower be," Edgar quietly quoted.

"Tha what?" asked Wick'un.

27

"Nowt," said Edgar. Wick'un looked at the old man who was gazing intently at the far wall. "Summat up?" he enquired.

"No, Ah were just thinkin' ov a chap from Elsinore," Edgar replied.

"Burnley way, is it?" Wick'un hazarded a guess, not having been much of a travelling man.

"Bit further than that," said Edgar, trying to marshal his thoughts. He sucked noisily at his moustache for a moment, before turning to Wick'un to say, "There's summat up when a chap goes into a pub an' t'landlord doesn't bother askin' if 'e wants owt to sup. Ah wouldn't mind a pint."

Wick'un strode off, muttering about whether or not he could remember how to pull a pint. He returned a few minutes later carrying two glasses, one of which he offered to Edgar, who, for some reason, was beaming with pleasure.

"Cheers," said the old man. "This un's on the 'ouse."

" 'Ey 'ang on a second," spluttered the landlord. "Ah've not forgotten everythin' tha knows. It's me as should say that!"

"Aye, tha's reet theer," said Edgar. "Tha should be sayin' it, 'cos Ah've getten a plan as should tickle thi fancy no end."

"Go on then," said Wick'un, lowering his hand which had been poised to take Edgar's money.

"Let's put it this way," said Edgar. "Today's Thursday, in't it? Now, if Ah can get thi pub filled tomorrer neet and packed o' Saturday neet, would that be worth a pound to thee?"

"O' course it would," responded the landlord.

"An' free beer an' brandy for me an' all?"

"Brandy?" queried Wick'un. "Tha durn't like brandy, tha calls it French.."

Edgar interrupted the landlord, "Never mind what Ah calls it, needs must when t'devil drives. Now, are thi gam for it?"

"Well, Ah durn't know," hesitated the landlord.

"See, if Ah durn't get thi some gradely trade in, Ah'll pay for all t'beer an' brandy an' tha can keep thi pound," offered Edgar.

"Ah'm gam," said Wick'un.

"I' that case Ah'll be off," said Edgar, finishing his beer. "Ah'll see thee later on, but mind, it'll be t'first time that tha's seen me today."

At half past nine, some two hours after Edgar had left the Holden Arms, only two more customers had entered. Slack Jack and Billy Shake-a-leg were regular clients who often drank as much as three halves apiece in a full night. However, what they lacked in ability or desire regarding the consumption of beer, they more than made up with by way of conversation, and even old women with less than an hour to spare, avoided them. Wick'un, pleased to have their custom, meagre as it was, tried valiantly to comprehend their inane dialogue.

"Ah've 'eard as t'leader o' Haslingden Temperance Brass Band were drunk as a mop in t'Clarence, last week," said Slack Jack.

"That durn't surprise me," replied Billy Shake-a-leg.

"Well, Ah'd a thowt it would 'ave, Billy. 'Im bein' drunk an' it bein' a temperance band an' all," said Slack Jack.

"Oh that bit surprises me," said Billy Shake-a-leg, adding, "Well it did when Ah 'eard it first ov all, not that it surprises me now like, 'cos Ah've 'ad time to get o'er me surprise. Nay, what Ah were referrin' to, when Ah said Ah weren't surprised, were what tha said about thee 'earin' about t'bandleader bein' drunk. Things like that get talked about so Ah weren't surprised when tha towd me that tha'd 'eard about it."

The two men paused to take the smallest of sips from their glasses. Wick'un also raised his glass, but this was more to cover his lips than to wet them, for unable to restrain himself, he gave vent to his thoughts, and with great feeling, he muttered, "What a load of horse manure." Fortunately for Wick'un, before the two men could enquire why he should have given utterance to that particular remark, the pub door flew open, and Edgar, hatless, sackless, and apparently witless, rushed up to the bar and cried out in a most piteous voice, "Wick'un, brandy, quick, gi' us a brandy." The landlord complied with this request in silence, as his tongue was clamped firmly between his teeth in order to prevent any untoward burst of laughter. Slack Jack was the first to comment on Edgar's appearance. "By gum Edgar, tha looks frozzen."

"Aye it is a bit parky out theer," offered Billy Shake-a-leg.

"It's not th' cowd as is mekkin me shiver," whispered Edgar, "Ah've just bin talkin' to Sammy Sup-all."

"Tha can't 'ave. 'E's bin dead ten year or more," scoffed Slack Jack.

"That's just what Ah towd 'im, but 'e'd 'ave none ov it," responded Edgar. Slack Jack and Billy Shake-a-leg were keen to know more and between them, they posed a dozen questions without waiting for a single answer. Wick'un, also eager to hear Edgar's story, took great pleasure in snapping at the two men, "Shut thi ruddy gobs an' lissen to th'owd chap!"

Edgar told his tale, supplementing it with much rolling of the eyes, several convulsions of the entire body and frequent pauses whilst his brandy glass was being re-filled. Within twenty minutes both Billy and Jack were fully convinced that Edgar had indeed been talking to the spirit of Sammy Sup-all, and even before he had finished his narrative they were mentally rehearsing their own versions of Edgar's experience.

"By gum, that's a tale an' an' 'alf," said Slack Jack, looking greatly impressed. He glanced at the clock on the wall, nudged his companion, and said with amazement, "Ee, look at t'time, we must be off now."

"Tha what?" queried Billy, who felt fairly snug where he was, and besides which, still had almost half of his second half left in his glass.

29

"Come on," said Slack Jack, giving his partner an imperious stare. Suddenly it dawned on Billy that there were people not yet abed to whom they could pass on the awesome tidings. "Aye," he said, "We'd best shake a leg." The two men, for the first time in many a year, hurried their beer without being asked and set off to spread the word. No sooner were they through the door than Edgar performed a glee-filled clog dance.

"Come on Wick'un, gi' us a pint. All that French water 'as given me an 'ell ov a thirst."

"Dost think as they believed thee?" asked the landlord as he pulled the drink. Edgar leaned across the bar to answer the question. "Proverbs, chapter fourteen, verse thirteen."

Wick'un showed some exasperation at this response. "Ever sin' tha sent that young curate packin', though only 'im, thee, t'vicar an' God knows 'ow tha managed it, tha's done nowt but quote t'Bible at me," said Wick'un, managing to mix two accusations in one, for Edgar had never revealed to him exactly what had transpired between him and the curate. "Just tell me what it says, but bowt t'numbers!" he snapped.

"It says," said Edgar, "The simple believeth every word." He sucked his moustache before adding, "An' there's none more simple than them two. Bi tomorrer dinnertime all o' t'valley'll 'ave 'eard an' bi tomorrer neet there'll be a swarm o' folks in 'ere, wantin' t'ear it from me own lips."

"Dost reckon?" Wick'un narrowed his eyes.

"What does ti reckon?" countered Edgar. Wick'un finished polishing the glass he was holding and put it back on the shelf. Straight-faced he stared at the old man for a few seconds before a small smile appeared.

"Wouldst like another when tha's finished that un?"

Despite four foot snow drifts and a blizzard, the Holden Arms was filled on Friday night, for Slack Jack and Billy Shake-a-leg had spared their tongues no effort in broadcasting their accounts of the previous evening, and as it was known that the Holden Arms was Edgar's second home, it was only natural that those desirous to hear Edgar's story first hand, should assemble there. At eight o' clock the old man appeared at the door, the cry went up, " 'E's 'ere," and a throng of people crowded around him.

"Gi' us a chance to get a pint in, will thee?" Edgar had to shout to make himself heard. He pushed his way to the bar where Wick'un and three barmaids were vigorously pulling pints.

"Bit busy toneet, Wick'un," said Edgar.

"Nay, just a normal neet, like any other," replied the landlord, thrusting two pints of beer into Edgar's hands.

Within a few minutes, Edgar, standing in front of the fire, had the undivided attention of everyone in the pub. He prefaced his story by explaining, for the benefit of those who might not have known, that the house he now lived in, had once been a beer-house, run by Sammy Sup-all who had died some years ago through an excess of drink. Then, in a fashion similar, though not quite as melodramatic, to the performance to Slack Jack and Billy Shake-a-leg, he recounted how, after having had his tea on the previous day, he had fallen asleep in his chair, only to be awakened by the sound of strange noises. On opening his eyes he had seen the disembodied spirit of Sammy Sup-all lifting a spectral beer barrel onto an equally spectral table. Edgar told his audience that when he challenged Sammy as to what he was up to, the dead landlord informed him that he was having a foot-in, or gathering, for his old friends.

"Well, Ah asked 'im oo 'e'd invited," said Edgar, "An' 'e tells me a list o' names o' chaps, an' they're all dead, so Ah says to 'im, 'Sammy, they're all dead, same as thee,' an' 'e says, 'Ah'm not dead,' an' Ah says, 'Tha're dead alreet, Sammy, Ah knows, 'cos Ah went to thi funeral,' an' 'e says to me, 'Were it a good do?' an' Ah thowt to missen, that's typical ov 'im is that." Edgar paused to take a mouthful of beer and then continued, "Ah durn't know why, but it were only then as Ah realised as Ah were talkin' to a ghost, despite the fact as Ah were lookin' straight through 'im so Ah thowt as best place for me is th'Olden Arms an' Ah gets down 'ere as fast as Ah could."

Edgar had been listened to in complete silence but as soon as he had finished speaking, a hail of questions were hurled at him and it became apparent that quite a number of the men were not convinced he was telling the truth. The debate continued until midnight at which time Edgar brought it to a conclusion by saying, "Reet, you lot, Ah've just remembered as Sammy towd me as this foot-in were to start at twelve o' clock toneet. Now then, Ah'm goin' 'ome to see what's 'appenin', an' if any o' thee wants to, tha can come wi' me."

"Well, Ah'd come if Ah could," said Wick'un, "but as tha can see, Ah'm a bit busy like." It was a very good excuse, but unfortunately for the others, not one which anyone else could use. It was one thing to mock the old man's tale in the warmth of the Holden Arms with the security of a number of friends, but to try to disprove him and thereby run the risk of seeing something unnatural was very much a different thing. Some rapid thinking ensued and a variety of reasons were given for their creators not being in a position or having the time to accompany Edgar to his home. Of all the multitude, only Dribblin' George, an habitual drunkard, was willing to co-investigate the matter. However, Wick'un gave the intrepid pair one for the road, a pint of beer for Edgar and a half pint of beer discreetly mixed with half a pint of whisky for Dribblin' George, who, in no time at all, was lying dead-drunk on the floor and showing as much animation as Edgar's sack. "Looks like tha're goin' 'ome on thi own after all, owd cock," someone shouted to Edgar.

"Aye," said the old man, slowly, "Ah suppose Ah'll see thee all tomorrer neet, God willin'," and stepped out into the wintery night.

At seven o' clock on Saturday evening Edgar arrived at the Holden Arms, which, even to his surprise, was already filled beyond capacity.

"What 'appened?" "Didst see Sammy Sup-all again?" Questions came from every direction, all of which the old man ignored until he had consumed three brandies and two pints of beer. "By 'eck, Ah needed that," he said, wiping his mouth with his coat sleeve.

"Tha saw summat then?" asked Wick'un.

"Saw summat? Saw summat? O' course Ah saw summat. Ah were theer wi' 'em for six 'ours or more," Edgar replied, haughtily.

"Oo were theer? Didst speak to any on 'em?" asked Slack Jack.

"Aye," said Edgar, picking up his third pint, "Ah spoke to some on 'em, an' by thump, Ah learned some stuff as ud mek thi 'air stan' on end." In fact some of the men surrounding Edgar could already feel their scalps prickling in anticipation of what Edgar might tell them, but as the comment had been made directly to Slack Jack, there was a small burst of laughter, it being well known that beneath his hat Slack Jack had not a strand of hair on his head other than the strong tufts which exuded from his nostrils and ears.

Edgar pushed his way to the fireside, turned to face his audience and proceeded to give a lengthy account of the main events and conversations of the foot-in which was attended by twenty men who had been deceased for as long, if not longer, than their host. Edgar's creativity, enhanced by alcohol, reached such incredible heights that eventually, one man, Owd Nat Barnes, a contemporary of Edgar's, could restrain himself no longer, and he shouted out for all to hear, "It's a reet load o' tripe, tha're mekkin' it all up."

From the expressions of those closest to him, Edgar could see this was a commonly held opinion. He had expected someone to make this accusation and to maintain his credibility, the first objector must be squashed so flat that none would dare to follow suit. Edgar had lived long and had travelled much in the area, picking up not only food for his belly and wood for the fire, but also knowledge of indiscretions, which he used for the occasional case of almost benign blackmail. He had however, come to learn of secrets so dark and terrible, that even he thought they should be kept forever, but in this instance, and having had good reason to harbour a grudge against Nat Barnes for over half a century, Edgar thought it fair and just, to shed a little light on a matter of history. For a second his thoughts flew back to when he was barely a boy, and he remembered himself in a dark, dank dungeon, talking for the last time to an old friend, who told him a story and then made him swear an oath never to reveal it. Edgar smiled, for after all, to tell a secret to a man who already knew it, was not the same as telling it to the whole world.

Edgar turned to the fire and warmed his hands, rubbing them together. He realised that the murmur of voices in agreement to Owd Nat's suggestion that there was no substance to his story, had now become an open conversation.

Edgar looked over his shoulder at his accuser and said, "Well, Nathaniel Barnes, Ah'll tell thee oo else were theer, an' that's 'Arry the 'Orse, 'im oo were 'ung for 'orse stealin' nigh on fifty year ago. 'E were a gradely chap were 'Arry, despite 'is wicked ways, an' 'e spared me a bob or two when Ah were a bit short." This was a slight exaggeration of Harry's generosity, for every shilling Edgar had received from him had been well earned, and, not without some little risk. Edgar continued, "Any'ow, Ah 'ad a natter wi' 'Arry, an' Ah can tell thee, it's a bit ov a bugger, tryin' to talk wi' someone oo's 'ead's all ov a tilt." He cocked his chin to one side, stuck his tongue out and opened his eyes wide, giving a passable imitation of a man who'd just been hung. "Now 'e 'ad summat reet strange to tell me did 'Arry, but it's a bit ov a secret, an' Ah can only tell one ov thee what it is." Edgar lost his smile, walked over to Owd Nat and said, "So Ah'll just tell thee, Nathaniel Barnes. Edgar stooped and in the man's ear whispered, " 'Arry towd me as 'e shouldn't 'ave bin 'ung on 'is own. 'E said as there were a young chap wi' 'im oo managed to get away when he were catched, but 'e didn't tell on this young feller, didn't 'Arry. 'No point i' both on us bein' 'ung for an owd nag,' says 'Arry. But after 'e'd 'ad 'is neck stretched, 'Arry found out as 'e didn't just stumble when 'e were tryin' to get away, the young chap as were wi' 'im 'ad tripped 'im up on purpose, to gi' 'imsel' a better chance o' scarperin'."

Edgar stood up and returned to his place by the fireside. The onlookers who had been watching Owd Nat's face saw it turn white then pale green. The man who only a few minutes ago had wind enough to scornfully mock Edgar now struggled for breath, and he raised a finger and ran it round the inside of his collar, as if loosening a rope from around his throat. From across the room Edgar barked, "Oo but a dead man could o' towd me that, Nathaniel Barnes?" Dumbstruck, Owd Nat could only shake his head in reply, desperately wishing he could rush out of the room but he was held back by the fear of what might be said about him should he leave. But Edgar held his piece on the matter, perfectly content at the way Owd Nat had reacted. The onlookers, having witnessed the way by which Edgar had silenced his first critic, thought it better to keep any lingering doubts they might have had to themselves.

Some hours later only Wick'un and Edgar remained in the pub, sitting contentedly by the fire and having their final drink of the evening.
"Bin a good neet for trade, 'as it?" asked Edgar, knowing full well it had.
"Not bad," replied the landlord who, having almost run out of beer on the previous night, had spent half the day visiting other landlords in the area, begging and borrowing extra barrels of beer, all of which were now empty. "Not bad," he repeated, and then finally conceded, "No, not bad at all."
"Glad about that," said Edgar, holding out his hand and smiling when Wick'un placed a pound note in it. The landlord pensively toyed with his glass for a

moment or two, trying to think of the right way to ask a question which no-one else that night had dared to ask Edgar. "Tha know," said Wick'un, "There were all sorts o' rumours goin' around after tha'd finished talkin' to Owd Nat. Some were sayin' one thing an' some were sayin' another. An' no matter oo asked 'im what tha towd 'im, th'owd feller wouldn't let on to nobody. Tha shut 'im up good an' proper, an' to tell thi t'truth, Ah've never sin a man look so fearful in all me life." Wick'un finally got round to his question. "What were it that tha said to 'im?"

"Nay Wick'un, Ah can't tell thee what Ah towd 'im," replied Edgar, "All Ah can say is... well let's put it this way..." but before he could complete what he was about to say, the landlord interrupted him by threatening, "If tha quotes Proverbs or Ecclesiastes or owt from t'Bible at me, Ah'll thump thee."

Unperturbed Edgar continued, "Ah were goin' to say as there's that owd sayin', 'It's not what tha knows that counts, but oo tha knows,' but to my way o' thinkin' it's what tha knows about oo that counts most."

An' that's the answer to me question, is it?" asked Wick'un. Edgar nodded. "Well," said the landlord, "Ignorance is bliss when tis folly to be wise, Ah suppose." And the old man smiled and nodded again.

AN IRISH HAYMAKER

Edgar felt he had done enough work for the morning, sufficient to justify a lunchtime drink. " 'Sides which, it's too 'ot," he muttered to himself. It was a warm day and the sun beat down on him, penetrating his overcoat, jacket, waistcoat, shirt, two vests and the remnants of a third, to an uncomfortable degree. He directed his footsteps to the Clarence, the nearest public house. He arrived there to find that all the downstair's windows were smashed, the glass still littering the pavement. He entered cautiously. The outward signs of disturbance were nothing compared to the devastation within. No table or chair had its full complement of legs, several doors hung off their hinges, broken beer glasses lay in the sawdust on the floor and the bar counter was tilted at a peculiar angle. Lying on the surface of a completely legless table was the landlord, undergoing treatment from a local physician.

"Alreet?" Edgar enquired of the prone figure.

"Don't be so ruddy gormless," snapped the landlord. "If Ah were alreet, t'ruddy doctor wouldn't be 'ere, would 'e?"

"Suppose not," said Edgar, airily. "What 'appened?"

"Finnigan," was the sole word in reply, but sufficient for Edgar to paint a full picture of the events in his mind's eye. Michael Finnigan, an Irish labourer, arrived every year for the hay-making season. For historical and personal reasons he had some cause for dislike of English landlords of the land-owning variety. Finnigan, however, refused to accept the difference between them and landlords of public-houses and considered anyone with the title to be a suitable object for his fists. After the hay-making and before moving on to pastures new, he would spend a few days in the vicinity with his compatriot workmates, getting drunk regularly and into fights occasionally. Wisely, Edgar had always kept clear of the marauders.

"Thy chaps must o' put up a gradely stand," observed Edgar, looking around the destroyed room.

"There weren't none ov 'em 'ere," growled the landlord. "Ah were on me own, so Finnigan sets about me, an' 'alf 'is mates, 'avin' no-one else to scrap wi' set about t'other 'alf."

35

Edgar turned the conversation to a more pressing matter, namely the likelihood of him getting a drink. The answer was an impolite refusal. He turned to leave but before reaching the door, he was called back by the landlord who said, "Tha'd best get word to Wick'un. Ah think Ah recall them Irishmen sayin' summat about goin' to th'Olden Arms toneet."

Edgar soon found another place of refreshment and whilst drinking his first pint, mulled over the news that he had just heard. He was always willing to make money as long as he didn't have to work for it, and a sixth sense told him that the present circumstances offered such an opportunity. Halfway through his second pint, he smiled and rubbed his hands.

For his plan to work, Edgar required the assistance of Tim o' Bob's. He sought the young giant at the timber yard where he worked and found him holding up the nearside of a fully laden cart, the wheel of which had fallen off and was currently being replaced by Joey Roses.

" 'Ow do, Edgar," said Tim, his voice showing no sign of exertion, despite the immense weight resting on his upturned forearms.

"Not so bad," replied Edgar, "but Wick'un might be 'avin' a bit ov a problem toneet. Can tha get up theer, 'bout six o' clock?"

"Aye," said Tim.

"Reet, Ah'll see thee then," said Edgar and left before he was asked to lend a hand.

The next step was, in Edgar's mind at least, no less dangerous than Daniel's confrontation with the lion; he had to find out if Finnigan was definitely going to the Holden Arms that evening, and at what time, and the only way to learn this was from the Irishman himself. The old man plodded around the town, and, after a few discreet enquiries, was informed that the Irish gang were presently lounging around on Duckworth's Field. It was there that Edgar found them, drinking, singing, cursing and fighting one another. He waited until there was a lull in their enjoyment before making his approach.

"Good afternoon, gentlemen," he offered. The men stared at him with great suspicion.

"Ah were wonderin' if Ah could 'ave a word wi' thee," said Edgar, taking a seat next to Finnigan, who possessed a barrel-like chest, arms as thick as a plump girl's waist and a neck that would have been a tight fit in a bull's halter. The fact that he was completely bald and wore a patch over one eye, or rather where the eye had been, made him even more recognisable by description.

"So you'd be wantin' a word wi' me, would you?" lilted the Irishman.

"Aye, but Ah thinks as we'd best 'ave a sup o' summat first," replied Edgar. He delved into his sack and pulled out a bundle of newspaper and cauliflower leaves, from the centre of which he extracted a bottle and passed it to the Irishman.

"A noice looking bottle, but short of a label," drawled Finnigan, before pulling out the cork. He took a careful sip, stared at Edgar for a second, and then took a large mouthful.

"Jaysus, the man who made that must have had lessons from an Oirishman," was the favourable comment which accompanied the sampling of Edgar's produce. Without compromising himself, Edgar gracefully accepted the compliment, and the ice thus broken, spent a congenial hour with the Irish contingent. He learned that they were indeed going to visit the Holden Arms that night and Finnigan, if he was in the mood, would 'request the landlord to engage in a gentlemanly bout of fisticuffs, just for the pleasure of it.'

" 'Ast ever sin 'im?" Edgar asked the Irishman, who looked nonplussed at the question.

"Would you be so koind as to repeat that question either in English or Gaelic and give me a chance to understand what you are asking?"

" 'Ave you ever sin, 'im, this landlord?" Edgar enunciated the words carefully.

"No, Oi haven't as a matter of fact, but that doesn't make any difference. If Oi feel loike foightin' him Oi will, and if Oi don't, Oi won't." This last statement was greeted by a series of loud guffaws from Finnigan's friends, giving Edgar the impression that it would be a cold day in Hades before Finnigan declined an opportunity to fight an English landlord.

"Ah bet thee a pound tha don't," said Edgar, fingers crossed. Finnigan's eye wandered over Edgar's shabby apparel, taking in the well-worn and badly-patched coat and trousers. "And would you be having a pound, then?" he asked.

"Aye," replied the old man.

"Well, Oi tink you'll be short of it by ten o' clock tonoight, or me name's not Michael Finnigan," boasted the Irishman. Edgar went home, suitably satisfied by the acceptance of the wager. After a short rest, he set off to meet Tim o' Bob's outside the Holden Arms at the appointed hour and they entered the pub together.

"Oy, Wick'un," Edgar shouted, " 'ow would tha feel if Ah towd thee as there's a dozen chaps on their way 'ere toneet as can all sup twenty pints apiece in less than an 'our?"

"It'd suit me down to t'ground," beamed Wick'un.

"Ah'm glad about that," Edgar beamed back, " 'cos Mick Finnigan and 'is chums are on their way."

The landlord stood in stunned silence for a second before he panicked.

"Oh nay, oh no, oh by 'eck!" He retreated behind the bar, pulled the hatch down and pressed his hands upon it, as if that would be sufficient defence against the Irishman's onslaught. Edgar and Tim shook their heads slowly.

"Oh, what'll Ah do?" whispered the landlord, wide-eyed with fear. "Ah suppose Ah could round up a load o' chaps an' get 'em to gi' us an' 'and in feightin' 'em off."

"What's ta mean, us?" asked Edgar.

"Tha wouldn't desert me in a time o' need, would tha?" whined Wick'un, looking suitably shocked that Edgar might even think of neglecting his duty to an old and trusted friend.

"Nay, o' course we wouldn't," said Edgar, "but thing is, Ah'm not as good wi me fists as Ah used to be, an' Tim 'ere durn't like to get involved in feights. Though we would if we 'ad to, wouldn't we Tim?"

"Ah suppose so," said Tim, reluctantly. "Though Ah promised me mother as Ah wouldn't get into any scraps. As Ah think Ah've towd thee she were on her..." Edgar interrupted Tim's explanation regarding the origins of his promise. "No need to tell me again," said Edgar, wanting to get on with the setting of his plan. "Nay Wick'un, there's no doubt about it, we'd be pleased to gi' thee all t'support tha needed in that direction, but just think on for a second, 'ow much damage twenty or thirty chaps all feightin' 'ud cause in 'ere. Ah saw what they did to t'Clarence, an' by 'eck, it'd bring tears to me eyes if that 'appened 'ere." Wick'un closed his eyes and imagined what the bar might look like. He shuddered. "What can Ah do?" he groaned, clutching the top of his head with both hands.

"Well, to be 'onest, Ah've bin givin' it some thought sin' Ah 'eard that Finnigan were on 'is way, an' Ah think Ah've getten an answer," said Edgar.

"What is it? What is it? Tell me quick."

"Cost thee two pound to find that out," said Edgar with a smile which expanded even more when two pound notes were thrust into his hand. Edgar carefully checked that there were not less than two, then slid one into his pocket, and passed the other to Tim o' Bob's.

"What's this for?" asked Tim, with some surprise.

"Wages," said Edgar.

"Eh?" said Tim and Wick'un together.

"It's simple enough," replied Edgar. "Tim, tha's towd me often enough as tha's always fancied being a publican, 'aven't tha?"

"Aye, true enough," said Tim.

"Well, toneet's tha chance to see what it's like. All tha's got to do is pretend as tha're Wick'un an' 'e's t'potman."

"Aye, alreet," said Tim. "But, 'ang on, just a second. If that Irishman's comin' up t'ave a feight wi Wick'un, don't tha think as 'e' might get confused a bit an' start scrappin' wi' me instead? Ah durn't want to go gettin' into no scraps. Ah durn't want to go 'urtin' no-one."

Edgar looked Tim in the face. "Tim, Ah promise thee, no-one's goin' to get 'urt," vowed Edgar.

"Oh that's alreet then," said the giant. It was alright by Wick'un as well.

The three men waited in silence, Wick'un sweating profusely, Edgar turning and twisting the pound note in his pocket, hoping that it would still be there at the end of the night, and Tim o' Bob's frowning. The cause for his consternation was a decision he had to make as to whether or not he should buy a kitten for his elderly aunt whose birthday was due the following week. On the one hand, her house was over-run by mice, but on the other hand, she didn't like cats. Then again, she didn't seem to mind the mice, but his mother did. She liked going to visit her sister but didn't like sitting on a sofa filled with nesting mice. He thought that his aunt might get used to the cat quicker than his mother would get used to the mice, but he wasn't sure and it was a vexing problem.

Tim's debut as a landlord was somewhat marred by the fact that other than Wick'un and Edgar, there was no-one for him to serve, for every time a regular customer arrived Edgar would send them on their way by saying, "Did tha know as Finnigan's on 'is way 'ere." The first time this had happened Wick'un had bitterly complained, "Don't tell 'em that, they'll all go away!" Edgar had sighed, "Aye, but think what'll 'appen if one ov 'em stays an' then lets slip to th'Irishman as Tim o' Bob's is pretendin' to be thee an' tha're pretendin' to be t'potman." The landlord paled and refrained from further comment until another ten minutes had passed when a sudden and terrible thought entered his head. "Oy, Ah've bin thinkin'," he said worriedly. "What if Finnigan already knows what Ah look like? 'E'll be able to tell as Ah'm not me."

"Nay, don't fret about that," said Edgar. " 'E's never sin thee."

" 'Ow does tha know?" asked Wick'un.

" 'Cos Ah 'ad a chat wi' 'im this afternoon, that's 'ow," replied Edgar.

"What's tha mean, tha 'ad a chat wi 'im?" Wick'un queried with more than a little anger in his voice. "An' what does tha mean, this afternoon? 'Ow long's tha known as Finnigan were on 'is way 'ere?"

Edgar quietly cursed himself for his mistake in letting the landlord know that he had conversed with the Irishman. However, he'd already realised that the landlord of the Clarence would sometime in the future let Wick'un know that he had tried to forewarn him of the impending visit. Edgar had wanted to choose the moment for revealing this but the time had arrived sooner than he'd expected. He decided to be brazen about it, and said, as if it made no difference, "Oh, Ah've known sin dinnertime as 'e were on his way."

"Tha what?" spluttered Wick'un. "Why didn't tha tell me sooner?"

"Nay," said Edgar, "Ah couldn't for shame 'ave towd thee before Ah did. Tha'd 'ave bin worryin' all afternoon."

"Ah ruddy wouldn't," hissed the landlord. "Ah'd a bin in Blackpool bi now!"

"Aye, an' worryin' thissel sick about what were goin' on whilst tha were away," replied Edgar. "Tha'd be frettin' thissel to death, wonderin' if tha'd a pub to come back to, wouldn't tha?" The landlord had to concede that this would probably have been the case. "Ah suppose tha're reet," he growled. Edgar scratched his chin, thoughtfully. Now that he had Wick'un slightly on the defensive, he thought it worthwhile to mention another small matter.

"Ah'm glad that tha brought up t'fact as Ah knew as Finnigan were on 'is way, 'cos after Ah found out, Ah thowt to missel' that t'best thing to do 'ud be to go and learn what 'e were up to, so Ah went an' 'ad a natter wi' 'im, an' that's when 'e towd me as 'e'd never sin thee before." Edgar scratched his nose before continuing, "Mind thee, Ah 'ad to gi' 'im a bottle o' me best whisky to loosen 'is tongue like." Then he added, generously, "But it's alreet, tha can pay me for it tomorrer." Wick'un narrowed his eyes. "If Ah'm still in one piece tomorrer to consider it, then Ah'll consider it." This brought the conversation to a close and silence reigned until half past eight when Finnigan and a dozen friends marched noisily into the pub.

"Evenin', Mister Finnigan," said Edgar, amiably, unnecessarily shifting to one side to make room for the Irishman. The latter leaned on the bar and looked at the man behind it, accurately estimating him to be slightly over six feet six inches in height and slightly less than twenty stone in weight.

"And would you be the landlord of this foine establishment?"

"Aye," said Tim, with his fingers crossed. He didn't like telling lies. "What's tha want to sup?" he asked, doing his best to mimic a good landlord.

"That's koind of you to ask," replied Finnigan, amiably. "Oi'd loike tirteen points of best bitter for me and me friends."

Tim started to pull the pints, but as he did so, he shook his head dubiously. "It's an unlucky number that, tha knows. Thirteen."

"It is an' all, but who for, now that's the question," responded the Irishman, ominously.

The opportunity was too good for Edgar to miss. "Tha could buy me a pint an' all. That'd mek it fourteen."

"Would that be suiting you better, landlord?" asked Finnigan, with a gentle smile.

Tim nodded and smiled back. Edgar and Finnigan were the last to be served with their drinks. As Tim put down the glasses in front of them, he commented on Finnigan's eyepatch.

"Got a bad eye, then?" Finnigan's disability was a touchy subject with him and even his best friends knew better than to mention it. His genial air disappeared briefly before he answered, "No, but Oi've got a good one." Edgar sensed a touch of malice and thought it high time that part three of his plan should be put into operation. This was to be a demonstration to the Irishman of Tim's pure indestructibility and total indifference to pain. There was a small risk to this as he had neglected to pre-warn the young giant of the test.

"Landlord," said Edgar. Tim looked towards Wick'un who was standing well out of harm's way.

"Landlord," said Edgar, glaring at Tim.

"Oh, aye, that's me," said Tim, suddenly realising that he was being spoken to.

"Come 'ere a tick, will ti?" Edgar asked him.

40

Tim stepped through the hatchway and stood next to Edgar and Finnigan. "What's up Edgar?"

"Ah thowt so. There's a wasp on thi trousers," said Edgar, peering closely at Tim's left leg. Tim did not like wasps. He remained perfectly still and said, "Get it for me, will ti?"

Edgar gave Tim's shin a hefty blow with his clog. "Drat. Missed it," he muttered. " 'Ang on, see, theer it is, on thi shirt." Edgar picked up his walking stick and drove it like a bayonet into Tim's solar plexus. Edgar cursed, "Missed the little bugger again." His eyes followed an imaginary flight. "It's landed on thi 'ead now," he whispered to Tim, stepped behind him, raised the stick and brought it crashing down onto Tim's unprotected skull.

"Didst get it then?" asked Tim, who hadn't moved an inch or batted an eyelid since the commencement of the old man's assault.

"Ah did that, landlord," replied Edgar happily, for he had been carefully monitoring Finnigan's reaction to the events and was pleased to see that a look of concern had settled on the Irishman's face.

But it was soon to be Edgar's turn to be concerned for Finnigan stepped forward and said, "Hold on there, landlord, Oi tink the little feller's missed it again. Aye, to be sure, there it is, the wasp's perched on your chin. But don't you worry none, Oi'll sort it out for you." Edgar held his breath and clutched his pound note.

Twenty-five Irish eyes were smiling as the Irishman took up a boxing stance. The punch was perfect, the surge of power behind it started in Finnigan's toes, travelled through his leg, up his back, across his shoulders and along his arm, culminating in a blur of fist which landed slightly to the left of the tip of Tim's jawbone.

Tim gently wiped his chin with his finger which he inspected for any possible remaining evidence of the insect. "Did tha get it?" he asked.

Finnigan eyed him with disbelief for a few seconds before answering, "Oi did that, and Oi can tell for sure, it won't be troublin' you again tonoight, nor will anything else." The latter part of the sentence being directed more to the gang behind him than to Tim.

Edgar moved closer to the Irishman and gave him a nudge and a quizzical look. The pound in his pocket was discreetly joined by another.

"As the Good Book ses, Proverbs, chapter three, verse ten, 'Strive not wi a man wi'out cause, if 'e 'ath done thee no 'arm,' or summat like that," quoted Edgar. The whispered reply slid from Finnigan's lips, "Between you and me and the Good Book, the big feller actually has done me some harm. Oi've at least two broken knuckles in me roight hand, but there's no need to tell him that."

"Fair enough," said Edgar. What Tim didn't know, wouldn't hurt him.

❖   ❖   ❖   ❖   ❖

41

A CART AND A FIDDLE

Edgar forced his way through the crowd and found his usual stool by the bar. Normally he was one of the first to cross the threshold of the Holden Arms but he'd dined well and had lingered at the table.

"Pint, Wick'un," he called out.

"Evenin' Edgar," said the landlord, putting a drink in front of the old man. He continued, "Jack, 'ere, were just tellin' us 'ow 'e peppered some chicken thief last neet."

Edgar turned to the man on his left.

"Evenin', Jack. What's all this then?" he asked. A broad shouldered man, with an evil glint in his eye, answered the question. "About three o' clock this mornin' there were some bugger after me chickens. Ah thowt it were a fox at first so Ah gets me gun an' goes out an' Ah spots this bugger runnin' across t'field like Owd Nick 'imsel' were after 'im. By gum, 'e couldn't 'alf clog it but Ah still managed to gi' 'im a backside full o' lead. Flat on 'is face 'e went, but up an' off again in a flash 'e were. T'bugger didn't get none o' me chickens though." The evil glint grew stronger and a malevolent smile creased the man's mouth. Edgar shook his head and tutted, "Tha can't trust anyone nowadays, can tha?" He ruminated on the fact that the farmer himself was something of a liar. Edgar knew for a certainty that the thief had not been hit by the shotgun blast but had slipped on the wet grass and the only damage sustained was a faceful of cowdung, more than compensated by a bellyful of chicken, which also proved the falsehood of the farmer's last statement. Edgar's tongue tried to dislodge a piece of chicken trapped between his teeth as he asked another question. "What brings thee in 'ere? Dost think as tha might recognise oo were after thi birds?"

"Nay, it were too dark to see oo it were," came the reply. "Ah've come down to see George Duck'orth. Ah wants a cart mekkin' for t'Misses."

"Tha'll be lucky," said Wick'un, "Grumblin' George'll not be mekkin' nowt for nobody. Towd me so 'imsel' last week. 'Is rheumatics 'as finally got t'better on 'im."

"Thump me," snapped the farmer. Edgar assaulted the piece of chicken with his fingernail. "Ah could mek thee a cart, as good as what Grumblin' George could," he announced.

42

"Thee? Mek a cart? Tha must be jokin'," scoffed the farmer.

"Ah'm not," said Edgar, haughtily. "Ah med one for Tom o' Dicks." He called out to a man at the far end of the bar. " 'Oy, Tom, 'ow's that cart o' thine?"

"Alreet," came the reply.

"Oo med it for thee?" asked Edgar.

"Tha did, tha cloth-heyd. 'Asta forgetten?"

Edgar had not forgotten, or rather, had not forgotten who he'd told Tom o' Dicks had made the cart. It had in fact been constructed by Grumblin' George. The buyer and seller of this particular cart had been, and still were, deadly enemies, and it was only through Edgar's secret involvement that the two men had been brought together in the transaction.

Jack left Edgar and went to have a discussion with Tom o' Dicks to find out more about Edgar's cartmanship. A few minutes later he returned, impressed, as Edgar knew he would be, for Grumblin' George was a rattling good cartmaker.

"Ah wants a cart for t'Misses," said the farmer. "Somethin' a bit fancy like an' Ah wants it a week before Walkin' Day." A price was settled upon and the farmer left, thinking he had got a bargain.

'A fancy cart for t'Misses, indeed,' thought Edgar. He could remember a time when Jack o' Livesey had nothing but a ragged shirt, torn britches and a pair of oversized clogs, all provided by the Overseer of Blackburn Workhouse when Jack had been put out to work for Tommy Ashworth. Edgar also remembered the wedding which had elevated Jack from the labouring ranks to a position of respectability. Tommy Ashworth, a widower, had a large farm and one daughter, Alice, the apple of her father's eye. The circumstances leading to the wedding had caused a number of surprises. Tommy was surprised that his daughter had managed to get herself a husband, for even he had to admit, despite his fondness for her, that she was not a comely maiden. Jack was surprised that Tommy hadn't blown his head off when he'd found that his daughter was with child. Alice was surprised that Jack hadn't run off when she'd told him of her condition. All the neighbourhood was surprised that Jack had ventured close enough to get her into that particular state, and even more surprised that after the wedding and the birth of the child, additions were made to the family at regular intervals.

Tommy Ashworth had died a few years later, and, having seen that Jack was capable of running the farm to his satisfaction, bequeathed it to him, rather than Alice. Edgar considered all this, and as he did not take too kindly to people who tried to shoot him, thought it might not go amiss to store up a few more surprises for Jack o' Livesey.

Wick'un, who had been called away to another customer returned to Edgar, leaned over the bar and whispered, "Are tha sure tha can mek a cart?"

"Speak up," said Edgar, "Ah think Ah'm goin' deaf in me reet ear." Wick'un peered under the brim of Edgar's hat. "Funny sort o' cure tha's getten for it," he observed, loudly.

"What's ta mean?" asked Edgar.

"Packin' thi lug 'ole full o' cowmuck, like," replied the landlord. Wick'un was polishing a glass with a tea towel which Edgar plucked out of his hand and used it to clear the blocked orifice. "Thanks," he said. "Don't mention it," muttered the landlord, who snatched back the cloth and continued to polish the glass, doing his best not to use the part which had been soiled.

Edgar had been given plenty of time in which to complete his task, but he set to work immediately. Within a few days, alerted by much banging, hammering and swearing, the neighbours soon realised that Edgar was building the cart in his parlour. News of this eccentricity travelled and a number of people sought out Edgar to discover how he intended to get the completed cart out of the house, the doorways of which were narrower than any cart they had ever seen. Edgar kept the sacks at his windows firmly drawn and refused to let anyone cross his threshold. In the Holden Arms, despite being plied with free beer, he steadfastly refused to answer the question of how he would get the vehicle onto the open road. Even Jack o' Livesey's questions remained unanswered.

After a few weeks, interest in the topic waned and Edgar decided it was high time for him to regain the attention of the public. One Saturday night, sitting on his stool in the Holden Arms, he remarked, "It's a fine lookin' cart for a fine lookin' lady," and accompanied the statement with a lecherous grin and a broad wink. Thus was started the rumour that Edgar and Alice were 'bothering'. Why else would Edgar, who'd barely done a stroke of honest work in his life, be spending so much time and effort on building a simple cart. And Jack was out in the fields all day. And, although Edgar was no picture, neither was the lady, it commonly being suggested that her distant parentage included a pig and a gargoyle. The story grew in the telling, and by the time it had reached Jack's ears, Alice's lastborn was reputed to have more than a passing likeness to Owd Edgar.

Jack o' Livesey, a possessive man, was not too pleased when he heard the slanderous accusation and immediately set off to discuss the matter with Edgar. He found the old man in the Holden Arms, or rather, just entering it from the yard containing the water closet. In no time at all Edgar had been forcibly returned to the small cubicle.

"What's all this about thee an' me Misses?" roared the farmer, as, with fingers firmly gripping Edgar's neck, he tried to thrust his captive head first into the odorous pit. Fortunately for Edgar, the wooden seat was down and its aperture was too small for his shoulders to pass through. Even more fortunately, Tim o' Bob's was soon on the scene and the young giant, with no visible effort, dragged the two men out and held them apart.

"What's up wi' thee?" Edgar asked, massaging his neck.

"Tha knows! What tha's bin sayin' about me Misses and thee, that's what's up!" hissed the farmer. Edgar pleaded ignorance. "Ah durn't know what tha's on about. All Ah've ever said is as Ah've bin mekkin' a fine looking cart for a fine looking lady." Edgar challenged the ensemble of drinkers, "Can any on thi say as Ah've said owt different?"

"Ah've never 'eard 'im say owt untoward about Alice," said Wick'un, shaking his head.

"Nor me," said Tim o' Bob's.

The farmer's anger subsided to a degree which Tim o' Bob's thought safe enough for him to release the man from his grasp.

"Tha shouldn't pay no 'eed to idle gossip," Edgar advised Jack o' Livesey. "Whoever started it all were doin' nowt but malicious slandermongerin". An' by t'way, t'cart's ready for thi Misses."

The farmer stared at the old man. "Ah think we'd best 'ave a word about that," he said. The two men went to a quiet corner of the pub. "After all t'trouble it's caused, Ah durn't think as Ah should tek this cart for t'Misses." Edgar was pleased with the man's statement, for if it hadn't been made, he would have had to bring up the subject himself.

"Ah can see thi point," he said. "It'd look reet bad, thy Misses ridin' around in a cart what Ah've med, it'd only start tongues waggin' again."

"Ah'm glad tha agrees wi' me," said the farmer, looking relieved.

"Aye," smiled Edgar, "as long as tha pays me for it, it can stay where it is."

The farmer didn't want to pay for something he couldn't use, and stated so, in no uncertain terms. "Any'ow, tha could sell it to somebody else."

"So Ah could," replied Edgar, "but think on what folks'll say when they see it bein' driven round town. 'Theer's that cart as Owd Edgar med for Jack o' Livesey's Misses,' that's what they'll say, an' a bit more an' all, Ah wouldn't wonder." The farmer winced at the thought of more gossip. He and Edgar haggled. Edgar wanted the full price of the cart as originally agreed. The farmer was willing to pay half. They settled on three quarters. Money, reluctantly given, enthusiastically received, exchanged hands. Jack stomped off home and Edgar sauntered gleefully to the bar where he proceeded to part with his earnings by buying a drink for Tim o' Bob's whose uninvited assistance had been a most timely blessing.

The week passed and Walking Day arrived, the first Sunday in May, when the congregations of the churches formed processions and marched round their parishes. It was a day for celebration and columns of joyous people, dressed in their Sunday best, followed the band, the choir and the vicar, who led the gay parade along the middle of the road. Those with fewer religious convictions walked on the pavement, keeping abreast of the procession. St. Stephen's had a good turn out, and, with onlookers, mustered over five hundred participants, all of whom had to pass Edgar's house. All of them saw the old man sitting on his garden wall, violently playing an horrendous tune on an old violin. All of them saw the board on which was scrawled, 'A penny a peek' accompanied by a drawing depicting a cart. Over the past few months the cart had been the source of much amusement and to actually see it was well worth a penny. Within a few minutes the vicar found himself at the head of a much diminished parade and Edgar found himself innundated with people, all of whom were pressing pennies into his hand for the privilege of peering in through his doorway. They couldn't see a great deal, for Edgar had carefully tied the door with string so that it would not open more than a few inches. Sacks still covered the windows but even in the gloom they could see well enough to observe a gaily coloured, full-sized cart standing in the room, almost filling it.

The public viewing refuelled the topic of how Edgar would get the cart out of his house. It was obviously too big to pass through either the door or the window, even if the window-frame itself was removed. The only alternative would be to knock a hole in the wall of the house, a potentially costly, and therefore unlikely possibility. Jim o' Kettlewell Hall summed up everyone's thoughts with the statement, "Yon's not goin' to get yon out o' yon in a month o' Sundays."

Gradually the throng of people rejoined the procession and Edgar was left alone. He rose, cut the string holding the door and stepped inside. From his sack he pulled a bottle of whisky, uncorked it and drank deeply.
"Cheers," he said, at the same time holding the bottle towards the cart. Whilst he admired the vehicle he counted the pennies he had just collected. He added the amount to the sum he had received from Jack o' Livesey and nodded his head with satisfaction. He estimated how much free beer he had been bought over the past few months and smiled. Putting the bottle down on the floor, he set to work. The wheels came off with only a gentle tug and he stood them against the wall ready to be returned to Grumblin' George from whom they had been borrowed. The body of the cart remained upright, supported by four wooden blocks, one of which Edgar kicked. The cart toppled and crashed against the wall. Constructed of cardboard and pieces of wood gathered by the old man on his travels, and only held together by two shillings worth of putty and lashings of paint, the cart crumpled with the impact. Edgar completed the destruction with his clogs and after a few minutes there remained nothing but a neat pile of irregular shaped sticks and a stack of paper. He picked up a few pieces of the wood, put them on the grate in the fireplace, and with a broad grin on his face muttered, "Ah'll bet not one ov 'em thought as Ah'd get thee out through t'chimney."

A WELCOME REPAST

The young man walked into the Holden Arms, approached the bar and ordered a pint of beer, adding, "My word, landlord, I'm rather hungry and there's a delicious smell coming from somewhere, what is it?"

"Me dinner," said Wick'un. "Meat pie, mashed spuds and black-eyed peys."

"Ooh," said the customer, licking his lips. " There wouldn't be enough for two by any chance, would there?"

"No," replied Wick'un.

"Well, I'd hate to deprive a man of his dinner," responded the young man, "but I am extremely hungry and I wonder if you might care to let me purchase your meal, for which I shall of course reward you handsomely."

"Three shillin's?" suggested Wick'un. "Willingly," said the young man, hastily paying for the food before Wick'un could change his mind.

"Ah'll go an' see 'ow it's doin', it shouldn't be long," said the landlord, as he walked into the kitchen and disappeared from view.

" 'Ow do," said Edgar, who was sitting at the far end of the bar.

"How do you do," came the polite response.

"Not bad, thanks for askin'," said the old man. "Tha knows," he continued, "that meal tha's just ordered reminds me ov a chap Ah once knew."

"Does it really?" asked the newcomer.

"Aye," said Edgar. "Dost mind if Ah tell thee about 'im, to pass the time like?"

"Be my guest," the young man answered, and Edgar, intending to be exactly that, commenced his tale.

"There used to be an owd couple, Edwin an' Sarah Barnes, as lived on Virgin's Row, just round t'corner from me. It were a neat little cottage they 'ad, two up two down, rooms downstairs bein' a bit ov a scullery where they did t'cooking and t'washin', and a parlour room as contained a black-leaded oven, one rockin' chair, two spindle backed chairs, an owd chaise-longue, a dresser, and a reet big wooden table as nearly filled t'room on its own. Now Edwin an' Sarah 'ad got more brothers an' sisters an' cousins an' nieces an' nephews than t'Royal Family, there were 'undreds of 'em, all spread out through t'valley. It so 'appened that one o' this clan, Uncle Billy who were retired an' lived in 'Aslingden, 'ad got into th'abit o' walkin' up t'Grane every Sat'day mornin' to see Edwin and Sarah. 'E were a big chap were Uncle Billy, fifteen stone if 'e were an ounce but 'e reckoned as this weekly stroll 'elped to keep 'im 'ealthy. Any'ow one particular mornin' he steps inside Edwin's cottage an' says, "By gum, that walk'll be t'death o' me yet," an' no sooner 'ad t'words come out ov 'is mouth than 'e proved 'is point bi droppin' down dead as a doornail on t'lino.

47

Well, like Ah said, 'e were a stout chap were Uncle Billy, an' th'owd couple 'ad a bit ov a problem in doin' summat wi' 'im, on account as they couldn't just leave 'im lyin' on t'floor. They started off by tryin' to lug 'im upstairs to t'back bedroom, but they weren't as young as they used to be an' couldn't even get 'im halfway up, so they give o'er on that idea. Then they plonked 'im on t'chaise longue but this weren't much cop of an idea neither, 'cos no matter which way they tried proppin' 'im up, he'd roll o'er an' fall off. They tried a few other things an' finally wi' a bit o' perseverance got 'im sorted out, but it 'ad tekken 'em all mornin' so they set about 'avin' some dinner. Whilst all this were 'appenin', Ah were recoverin' from a bad neet, an' not feelin' like cookin' for mesel', and knowin' as Edwin and Sarah were allus good for a bacon butty, Ah called in on 'em. Well, Ah walks in an' t'first thing Ah sees from t'door 'oyle is Billy laid out on t'table. Then Ah takes a closer look and sees as 'e's dead. " 'E's dead!" Ah says out loud, thinkin' Ah were talkin' to mesel'. Then Edwin and Sarah pop their 'eads up from t'other side o' Billy, an' Edwin says, wi' is gob full o' food, "Aye, 'e is," an' Ah realise as they're 'avin' their dinner. Now Ah'd noticed as they'd put a couple o' pennies on t'dead man's eyes, an' Ah don't blame 'em 'cos there's nowt worse than bein' stared at when tha're eatin'. Well, after they'd finished their dinner, an' were sidin' t'table, apart from Uncle Billy that is, Ah towd 'em as Ah'd always been fond o' th'owd chap an' Ah'd be grateful if Ah could pay me last respects to 'im there an' then, on me own like. Bein' good neighbours they said it were alreet an' both on 'em went into t'scullery, leavin' me alone wi Uncle Billy. Any'ow after a bit they come back in an' it weren't long afore they noticed as t'coins 'ad gone from Billy's eyes. They didn't 'alf moan at me an' Ah couldn't do nowt else but 'and o'er t'pennies as 'ad some 'ow slipped into me pocket. Tha wouldn't 'ave believed 'ow much fuss they med o'er tuppence! It suited me though, 'cos it stopped 'em from noticin' as Ah'd swapped boots wi' th'owd feller. These are them as Ah've getten on me feet reet now. They've done me proud 'ave these boots."

At this point Wick'un re-entered the bar, carrying a plateful of steaming food and Edgar concluded his tale by saying, "Aye, 'e 'ad a good set o' false teeth an' all, did Uncle Billy, but Ah wore them out years since."

Wick'un found it difficult to believe that a man who ten minutes before had been ravenously hungry should turn his nose up at the food now in front of him. "I'm sorry landlord, I seem to have lost my appetite," said the young man, faintly.

"Ah'll eat it for thee," Edgar volunteered and the young man immediately pushed the plate along the bar towards Edgar with one hand, the other being occupied in holding a hankerchief to his face.

"Aye," said the old man, with a mouthful of food. "This is exactly what Edwin an' Sarah were eatin' when Ah went in an' saw Uncle Billy laid out dead on their table; meat pie, mashed spuds an' black-eyed peys."